C000186830

POP

© Haynes Publishing, 2008

The right of Richard Havers to be identified as the author of this Work has been asserted by him in accordance with the Copyright, Designs & Patents Act 1988.

All rights reserved. No part of this publication may be reproduced, stored in a retrieval system or transmitted, in any form or by any means, electronic, mechanical, photocopying, recording or otherwise, without prior permission in writing from the publisher.

First published in 2008

A catalogue record for this book is available from the British Library

ISBN 978-1-84425-668-6

Published by Haynes Publishing, Sparkford, Yeovil,
Somerset BA22 7JJ, UK
Tel: 01963 442030 Fax: 01963 440001
Int. tel: +44 1963 442030 Int. fax: +44 1963 440001
E-mail: sales@haynes.co.uk
Website: www.haynes.co.uk

Haynes North America Inc., 861 Lawrence Drive,
Newbury Park, California 91320, USA

All images © Mirrorpix

Creative Director: Kevin Gardner
Packaged for Haynes by Green Umbrella Publishing

Printed and bound in Britain by J. H. Haynes & Co. Ltd.

POP

The Weird, the whacky, the wonderful
world of pop & rock

Richard Havers

'ROCK STAR DIES IN CAR CRASH

PICTURED LEFT: The

AMERICAN rock 'n' roll singing star Eddie Cochran, 21, died yesterday after a car taking him to London Airport crashed.

Among the three other passengers in the car were two Americans — "rock" singer Gene Vincent, and songwriter Sharon Sheeley, 20.

Sharon Sheeley

Mirror
34. Saturday, February 8, 1964 · No. 18,704

Fans on a roof at London Airport wave goodbye to the Beatles yesterday.

YEAH! YEAH! U.S.A!

That old Beatlemania hits New York as a screaming girl tries to reach the Beatles.

Paul, Ringo, George and John answer questions at the Press conference.

5,000 scream 'welcome' to the Beatles

FIVE thousand screaming, chanting teenagers — most of them playing truant from school — gave the Beatles a fantastic welcome here today.

More than 100 extra police were on duty to control the crowd at the John F. Kennedy Airport.

IRENE GOES HOME TODAY

PRINCESS Irene of Holland, whose romance has started a constitutional crisis, is going home today.

'Some good news soon'

Retreat

Overcome

Elvis Aron P...
BORN: Tupelo, Mississ...
January 8, 1935
DIED: Memphis, Tenne...
August 16, 197...

...tain—then the Big Hello

...ce at last

Friday, September 2, 1977

he troubleu

...death as he lay in a steel-...

Saturday May

McCartney sues Ringo, John and George

DAILY Mirror
6d. Friday, January 1, 1971 · No. 20,838

SPLIT UP THE BEATLES SAYS PAUL

BEATLE Paul McCartney is asking to break up the famous group.

He has issued in a High Court writ as 'caretaker' Receiver to be appointed as group's accountants.

He is also seeking a declaration that the partnership — the Beatles and Co.— formed in April 1967, ought to be...

Russia reprieves two Jews

RUSSIA yesterday reprieved two Jews...

The Mirror
www.mirror.co.uk

THANKS, F...

'You gotta love...
.. dying's a pai...

SINATRA TRIBUTE: PAGES 2, 3, 4...

JAGGER ...DDING DAY ...OUGH HOUSE

Mayor threatens to call it off

Welcome to today's winning Mirror

BUGNER

ANSWER BOO BO...

Sex a... chast... by p... age...

The Mirror
www.mirror.co.uk
Monday May 1 2000 · 32p

Help design Diana memorial
MIRROR READERS INVITED TO SEND IN THEIR IDEAS: PAGE 7

Racist scare Hague is new Enoch

MADONNA SACKS HER BUTLER

He will sue for £100,000

EXCLUSIVE

DAILY Mirror
FORWARD WITH BRITAIN · 18p

Great new competition next week
PLUS TODAY Four-page...

ELTON...

POP, POP, POP POP Music...

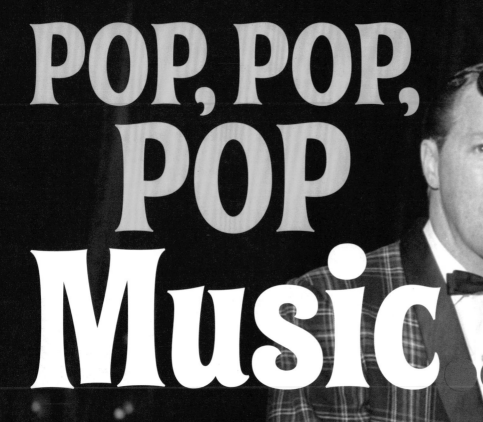

What is pop? Think about it for a moment. It's a sound, it's a kind of drink, it could be someone's father, it's movement – I'll just pop along, it can mean opening and shutting something and it's also short for popular. Since the 1950's it's been used in its abbreviated form to denote popular music. Before Bill Haley appeared on our shores popular music was much more refined – and of course controlled by those nice people at the British Broadcasting Corporation. 'The organist entertains in a thirty minute programme of today's most popular tunes.' Gradually things changed and before long in New York, London, Paris and Munich, everybody was talking about pop music....

Because it's short for popular music then what's to stop us including any kind of music in this book... absolutely nothing, say it again... absolutely nothing. The sad thing is as often as not 'Pop' is used in a kind

This book is here to celebrate pop music, to take a light-hearted, sometimes irreverent look at a business which occasionally takes itself seriously but mostly we're just, as Andrew Loog Oldham, the former manager of the Stones and founder of Immediate Records, said;

'Happy to be a part of the industry of human happiness.'

of dismissive way…oh that's just pop; it's as though other musical genres are far more important. Well here's something to mull over. Pop is the single most appreciated art form in the world today. What! We hear you say. How can that be? Well creating music is an art form, just as much as painting pictures, some of which may even be pop art, or sculpting or opera or classical music, or for that matter any other kind of art. Arguably more people appreciate pop music than all those art forms put together.

Here you'll find bubblegum pop, Brit pop, pop-rock, jangly pop, sub pop, sunshine pop, straight pop, pink pop; then there's all the other kinds of popular music. Rock, soul, R&B, blues, jazz, folk, rap, hip-hop – because if it's music that's popular, then it's POP. The fact is that it's usually people who want to differentiate their music from someone else's that love to put labels on things; it's a kind of musical class warfare. Our music's better than your music – plus the fact that marketing people love to put handles on everything. It makes selling the music to us all so much easier. Or does it?

Bill Haley and his Comets on stage

7th February 1957

"The rowdy element was represented by Rock Around The Clock, theme song of the controversial film Blackboard Jungle. The rock 'n' roll school in general concentrated on a minimum of melodic line and a maximum of rhythmic noise, deliberately competing with the artistic ideals of the jungle itself" – **Encyclopaedia Britannica appraising Rock 'n' Roll in 1955.**

From the Archives

Frank Sinatra

Frank Sinatra during rehearsals for a charity Midnight Matinee at the Coliseum on 9 December 1951. Frank was famous for his quotes.

"You only live once, and the way I live, once is enough."

"Thank you for letting me sing for you."

"Ladies and gentlemen, may you all live to be 102 years old and the last voice you hear be mine."

The Fifties Quiz

1. Who had the most British Top Ten records in the Fifties; Elvis Presley, Buddy Holly, Frankie Laine or Frank Sinatra?

2. What was Cliff Richard's first hit?

3. Who was the first British artist to top the US charts?

4. Three of the UK's Top Ten singles of all time – based on weeks on the chart – were released in the Fifties. Can you name the three artists who sang them?

5. The Fifties were a decade of the solo singer but five groups had No. 1 records during the decades – we're not thinking of duos here, but proper groups of three members or over?

6. Name the record that spent more weeks on the British singles chart in the Fifties than any other?

7. Whose record was topping the charts as the Fifties came to an end?

8. A BBC DJ whose career lasted into the 21st century topped the British charts in this decade, who was he?

9. Two pianists topped the charts in the Fifties, what are their names?

10. Who was the first black artist to top the British charts?

For the answers see page 208 where you'll also find the names of the performers pictured here.

From the *Archives*

The Stones at the Alamo in Texas in 1975, by which time everyone thought they were getting old. Little did they know! They were in for thirty-something more years of the 'Greatest Rock and Roll Band in the World'.

On Wednesday 4 June the Stones did this exclusive photo shoot for the Daily Mirror prior to playing a gig at the Hemisfair Arena in San Antonio, where they'd also played the night before. This was the first time the band had been back to the Texan city since a show at the State Fair in June 1964 on their very first tour of America; on that occasion they followed a bunch of performing monkeys and preceded Bobby Vee and his band.

In 1975 it was all very different, the Stones were banned from appearing on stage with a giant inflatable plastic penis and threatened with legal action by the police. According to Mick Jagger, 'It wasn't worth spending a night in jail for.'

Then & Later On
Kylie Minogue

How did cute little nineteen-year-old Kylie go from this in 1988 to this in 2003? When the first picture was taken she'd just made No. 1 with I Should Be So Lucky, her first UK single having been signed up after singing Little Eva's old hit The Loco-Motion on Neighbours the Aussie soap; a version of which topped the Australian charts for seven weeks and made No. 2 when it was released in Britain. Her first UK single stayed at No. 1 for five weeks – those were the days when records lasted more than a week at the top. In the next two decades she's had five more records topping the singles charts and countless other British Top Ten hits.

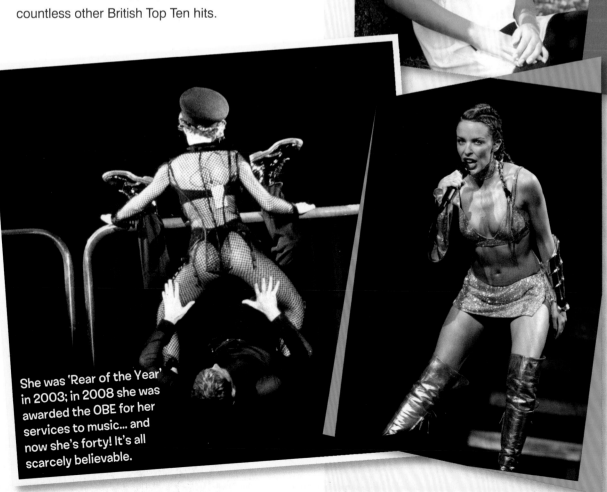

She was 'Rear of the Year' in 2003; in 2008 she was awarded the OBE for her services to music... and now she's forty! It's all scarcely believable.

Barry (right) with Robin (centre) and Maurice in 1989.

Top 10 hits

written by the brothers Gibb

Between them Barry, Robin and Maurice have been a formidable hit factory over the years. Other than Lennon and McCartney no other band has written more hits for other people than The Bee Gees. Besides Massachusetts they wrote four other No. 1s for themselves; in America they've topped the Hot 100 eight times.

1. **Massachusetts** – The Bee Gees – UK 1967
2. **If I Can't Have You** – Yvonne Elliman – US 1978
3. **I Just Want To Be our Everything** – Andy Gibb – US 1977
4. **Love Is Thicker Than Water** – Andy Gibb – US 1978
5. **Shadow Dancing** – Andy Gibb – US 1978
6. **Grease** – Frankie Valli – US 1978
7. **Woman In Love** – Barbra Streisand – UK & US 1980
8. **Islands In The Stream** – Kenny Rogers & Dolly Parton – US 1983
9. **Chain Reaction** – Diana Ross – UK 1986
10. **How Deep Is Your Love** – Take That – UK 1996

Tragically Andy Gibb died aged thirty from an inflamed heart.

Dolly in 2002 performing one of her many greatest hits...

The 80s
Revisited

Why is Rick Astley trying to put his finger up Marti Pellow's nose? Does Marti like things up his nose? The two singers were at the Limelight Club in London and Rick's song, Never Gonna Give You Up was at No. 1 – his first, and so far, only record to top the charts, which may explain his slightly odd behaviour; that and what may be a glass of orange juice in his hand.

Rick with record producers Mike Stock, Matt Aitken and Pete Waterman who masterminded his success. There were six more UK Top Ten hits and then a host of minor singles. He's been back touring in the UK recently so who knows, there may be some more hit records.

Eric Burdon, the singer with The Animals married model Angela King at Caxton Hall in London in September 1967.

In December 1969 Dave Munden, the Tremeloes drummer, married 22-year-old Andre Wittenberg, a bunny girl from the Playboy Club in London. After the service they walked under an arch made up of Bunny girls holding up bunny tails. The Tremeloes, left to right: Chip Hawkins, Alan Blakley, the groom, and Rick West.

POP Weddings

Of course back in the Sixties it wasn't all free love among the pop glitterati; most self-respecting male pop stars married a model, or if they were in short supply a Playboy Bunny – some things don't change. Although these days footballers seem to have cornered the market on models.

Paul with Linda Eastman after their wedding ceremony lunch at the Ritz Hotel in March 1969.

In November 1969 the paper said 'Hit songwriter Graham Gouldman who has produced top ten numbers for The Hollies, Herman's Hermits and the Yardbirds, was married yesterday to Miss Susan Gottlieb, a jeweller's daughter, in Manchester. The couple are seen leaving the Holy Law Synagogue at Prestwich after the ceremony.' Later Graham formed 10CC who had a massive hit with I'm Not In Love.

Surprise, surprise, Cilla Black marries Bobby Willis at Marylebone Register Office in London in January 1969.

Lulu and Maurice Gibb of The Bee Gees get married in February 1969.

Singer Susan Maughan married London advertising executive Mr Nicholas Teller at Hampstead Register Office in June 1965.

Peter Noone, aka Herman of Herman's Hermits, married 22-year-old Mireille Strasser in November 1968.

OK; so this wasn't the Sixties but May 1970. However, saxophonist and organ player Graham Bond, with his high brown suede boots and a tabard, at the time was in Ginger Baker's Air Force married one of the band's singers, Diane Stewart, and they seem to capture the spirit of the age.

And finally a wedding that might not have been. . .

According to reports in November 1968. '30-year-old pop star P.J. Proby announced his engagement to British actress Vanessa Forsythe. He has two problems – he is £84,000 in debt and is unsure of the legal standing with his two previous wives. P.J. and his intended at his Hendon (that's not very rock 'n' roll – Ed) home.

It's the REAL THING
or is it?

Tribute Bands are big the world over, some like The Bootleg Beatles have probably played to more people than the originals did during their career. What's so great about them is not just their dedication to the cause but the creativity that goes into their names... some more than others!

Nearly Dan

Björn Again

The Bootleg Beatles

The B' Eagles

The Australian Pink Floyd Show

The Australian Doors Show

No Way Sis

The Counterfeit Stones (theirs was 'The Flyovers To Basildon' Tour)

Sticky Fingers (Dick Swagger & Keith Riffoff are two of the members)

AB/CD

Re-Genesis

Seismic Ring (Jethro Tull tribute band formed in Scunthorpe)

Who's Who

The Cosmic Charlies (Dead tribute)

The Backbeat Beatles

The L.A. Doors

Eton Rifles (The Jam)

Male Order

Purple Reign

Wonderwall

One Step Below (Madness)

Born Jovi

Whole Lotta Led

The Beached Boys

Lez Zeppelin – an all girl tribute band

Björn Again.

Young Debbie or Deborah as she later became.

The Ozmeister, taken in 1981, three years after the picture of Ms Harry.

Spot the
Oldie

Ok, it's competition time. Ozzy Osborne, Debbie Harry, Marianne Faithfull and Iggy Popp, who is the oldest? Answers on page 208.

Miss Faithfull in 1980 – it really is her real name! Not too difficult to see what a young Mick Jagger saw in her and he wasn't the only one. Apparently Robert Mitchum, Bob Dylan and Rod Stewart all tried, and failed, to have their wicked way with the lovely Marianne.

Iggy Pop in 1977.

1969 A Pop Oddity

In the spring of 1968 the ukulele-playing Tony Tim, whose real name was Herbert Khuary – maybe it wasn't a bad idea to change it in his quest for fame – stormed the American charts with his rendition of Tip-toe thru the tulips; although stormed maybe stretching a point as he only made No. 17. A few months later he got to No. 95 with his follow-up, then in 1969 his remake of Great Balls of Fire managed ten places higher. In Britain his career was even shorter with just one week on the charts with Great Balls, in early February. Undaunted, in 1969, his record company, Frank Sinatra's Reprise label, sent him over to London to try to drum up some business. He appeared at a charity 'Save Rave Pop Show' at the London Palladium, which Princess Margaret attended. According to the newspaper that day 'Tiny Tim will be wearing three neck ties given to him by his girl friend Miss Vicki, he will wear them all at once, when he goes to bed they go on his pillow.'

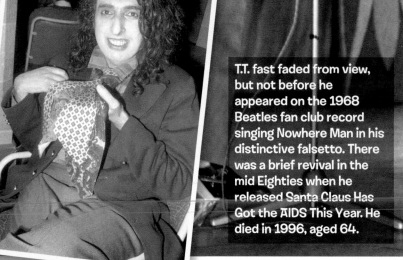

T.T. fast faded from view, but not before he appeared on the 1968 Beatles fan club record singing Nowhere Man in his distinctive falsetto. There was a brief revival in the mid Eighties when he released Santa Claus Has Got the AIDS This Year. He died in 1996, aged 64.

Lonnie Donegan

A man with a lot to answer for

Skiffle's superstar Lonnie Donegan had, between 1956 and 1962, thirty British hit singles; topping the charts three times as well as fourteen other Top Ten singles. His first hit, Rock Island Line, made the US Top 10 in 1956, a rare achievement for a British record.

Connected by Birth

Boney M.

Jerry Butler was born in Sunflower, a hit for Paul Weller.

Jerry's fellow Impression, Curtis Mayfield, was born in Chattanooga who's Cho Cho was made famous by Glenn Miller.

James Brown was born in Desdemona, a single release for Marc Bolan's group, John's Children.

Van Morrison was born in Belfast, a hit for Boney M.

Phil Everly was born in Chicago, a hit for Frank Sinatra.

Tony Orlando was born in Manhattan, a standard recorded by Ella Fitzgerald.

Dorothy Provine was born in Deadwood, The Deadwood Stage was a hit for Doris Day.

Glen Campbell was born in Delight, Arkansas. If it was in the afternoon then The Starland Vocal Band made the perfect record in 1976, Afternoon Delight.

Kim Carnes was born in Pasadena, which was a hit for the Temperance Seven in 1961.

Carole King was born in Brooklyn and Barry Manilow sang Brooklyn Blues, as he was also born there he should know.

Stevie Nicks was born in Phoenix a few years before Glen Campbell sang By The Time I Get To Phoenix.

Bill Medley of the Righteous Brothers was born in Santa Ana, California and The Beach Boys sang

Santa Ana Winds; there is no evidence that the song was about Bill.

Dusty Springfield was born in Hampstead and when the Dream Academy sang Hampstead Girl it was very definitely not about the greatest white soul singer ever.

Stevie Nicks.

Glen Campbell (right) with Scottish golfer Bernard Gallacher.

Doris Day.

Paul Weller.

Ella Fitzgerald.

Barry Manilow.

Van the Man.

Dusty Springfield.

Marc Bolan.

Music for Sophisticates!

For Just £46 Gns

This beautiful radiogram could be gracing your home.

With the capacity to play up to eight LPs one after the other through the medium of our almost unique auto-changer you can have two and a half hours of continuous music. You will never have to leave the dinner table to change a record and with a little pre-planning you and your guests will be able to enjoy just the right music to accompany your prawn cocktail or that cheese fondue with succulent roast beef.

Are you Listening?

Not unique among celebrities, but musicians have developed their very only sign language for dealing with unwanted attention.

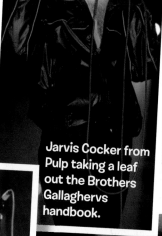

Jarvis Cocker from Pulp taking a leaf out the Brothers Gallaghervs handbook.

Keith from The Prodigy says Hello at Leeds.

Liam Gallagher of Oasis who has raised sign language to something of an art form.

Noel Gallagher, having possibly learned the technique from his brother takes it to its ultimate with the 'two-hander.'

You've just got to

Newspaper cartoonists look everywhere for inspiration, but it wasn't until The Beatles and the Stones came along that pop music became a regular and varied source of material. Stanley Franklin became the Daily Mirror's political cartoonist in 1959, staying there until 1970. He was around during the heyday of the rise and rise of pop and he was merciless in suing it to take the rise out of politicians and sometimes even pop stars.

This is the first mention of The Beatles, and came out as She Loves You was at No. 1.

The Beetles

'I thought it was the usual police escort'
FRANKLIN

From 6 July 1966 when The Beatles got into a row while in the Philippines on tour over an alleged snub of Imelda Marcos, the wife of the President – yes, she of the shoes fame.

31 December 1963. The Beatles and the Stones were fertile fodder for the cartoonists as they had long hair, so it became like a trademark motif. The first Stones cartoon to appear in a National newspaper was one of Franklin's and it perfectly illustrates the point. Of course now we just look at them and think how respectable they really appear.

"Thanks, fellows, it's all for a good cause."

Laugh...

DAILY MIRROR 13TH MAY 1964

'ROLLING STONES' POP GROUP REFUSED LUNCH. YOU MUST WEAR COLLAR AND TIE, SAY HOTEL MANAGEMENT

FRED'S CAFE

MENU
CHEESE ROLLS £2-10-0 EACH
TEA 15/- A CUP
FRUIT CAKE QUID A SLICE

FRANKLIN

"Crikey, your prices are up a bit since celebrities started dining 'ere, aren't they, Fred...?"

RUMOUR THAT THE ROLLING STONES POP GROUP ARE ENTERING A SHETLAND PONY

FRANKLIN

This classic from May 1964 strikes to the heart of what (old) people just couldn't stand about the Stones – they would not conform. Imagine going into a hotel restaurant without a jacket and tie! According to Bill Wyman, 'We met in the hotel's Cocktail Bar. Keith was wearing a sweater, Mick a striped sweatshirt and corduroy trousers, Stu a blue pullover, and Charlie and I were wearing coloured sweaters. We then went for lunch in Bristol's Grand Hotel restaurant, the Bordeaux Room. We were refused entry by the headwaiter and they offered us lightweight fawn jackets and maroon ties, but we walked out. We checked out, drove to the nearby Bali Restaurant and had a nice lunch of curried prawns and cokes.'

The introduction of the Marine Offences Act in August 1967 led to the demise of the pirate radio ships that had done so much to change the way young people in Britain listened to pop music. Radio 1 began broadcasting at the end of September and this is Franklin speculating on what might become of Radio Caroline, one of the most popular stations.

Radio Caroline to hold "French weeks" with programmes devoted to France.

FRANKLIN

"That new disc jockey's been playing 'The Marseillaise' non-stop for three days now."

Pop stars and their Cars!

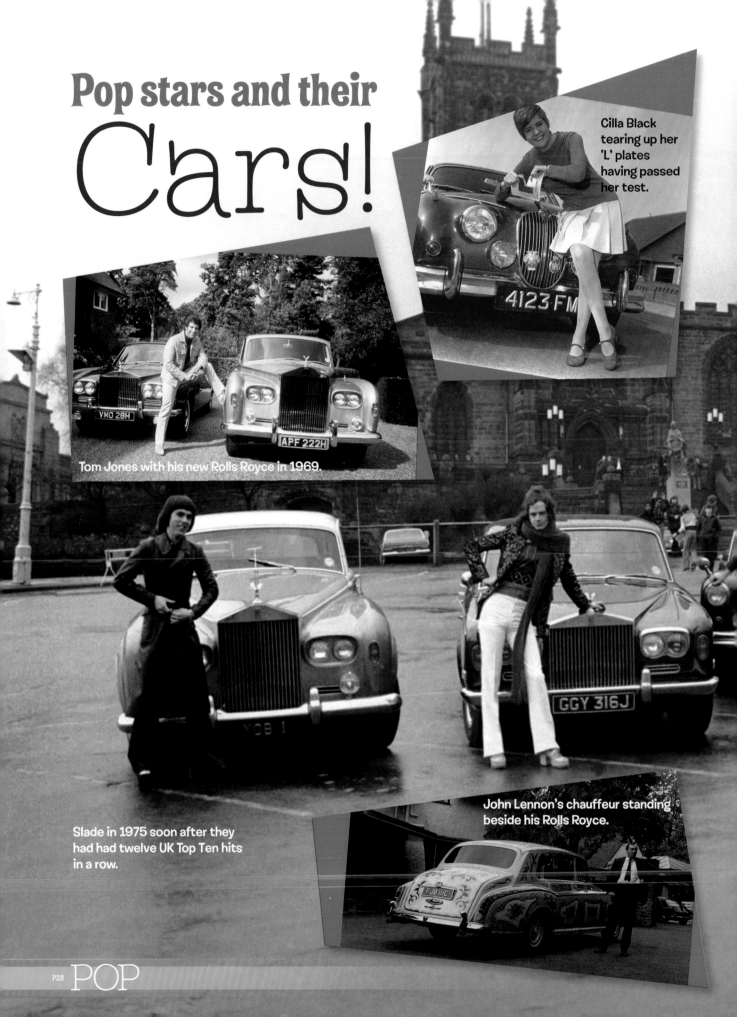

Cilla Black tearing up her 'L' plates having passed her test.

Tom Jones with his new Rolls Royce in 1969.

Slade in 1975 soon after they had had twelve UK Top Ten hits in a row.

John Lennon's chauffeur standing beside his Rolls Royce.

Tommy Steele at home with his new £3,700 Mercedes Benz sports car.

Mel B of the Spice Girls.

In August 1966 Mick Jagger crashed his midnight blue Aston Martin DB6. Mick's girlfriend, Chrissie Shrimpton, looks on as the patrolman takes his particulars.

Sadly Cliff just had a bus for going on his summer holidays.

HEAVY METAL
Madness on the
Highway to Hell

OLD ROCKERS JUST LOVE TO POSE.

Lemmy from Motorhead in 2002 – this is possibly the same bottle of Jack Daniels that Keith Richards uses for photo shoots.

David Coverdale of Whitesnake in 2006.

Motorhead in 1984 inexplicably burning one of their own...

Kirk Hammett and Lars Ulrich of Metallica in 1996.

Deep Purple before they got very heavy.

Kiss at Heathrow in 1980.

Iron Maiden in Rome in 1980. Shades, faded denim, the hair, mostly black, tattoos – not a lot missing...

Have you ever pondered why you've never seen Jethro Tull and the Time Team presenters together, in the same place, at the same time?

Axel Rose of Guns N' Roses wants to be taken seriously...

The 80s
Revisited

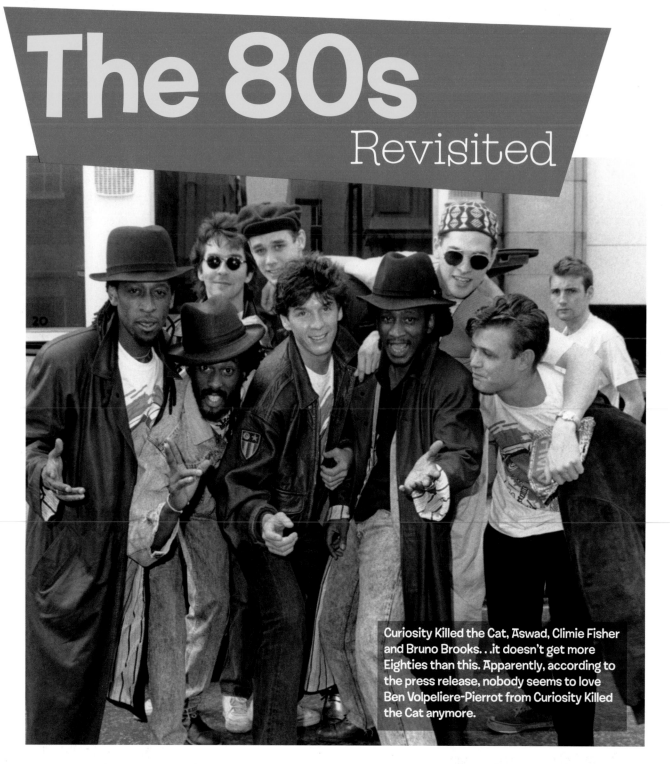

Curiosity Killed the Cat, Aswad, Climie Fisher and Bruno Brooks. . .it doesn't get more Eighties than this. Apparently, according to the press release, nobody seems to love Ben Volpeliere-Pierrot from Curiosity Killed the Cat anymore.

Last weekend (it was May 1988) the generous singer took part in a charity event, filling dustbins with albums to raise £9,000 for the Thames TV Telethon. Co-contestants Aswad and Climie Fisher then came up with the bright idea of kidnapping Ben to raise more cash. The unsuspecting singer was bound, gagged and whisked off to a derelict house in Brixton. Simon Climie and the Aswad lads then rang Ben's record company seeking £10,000 for his return – 'Keep him – he's not worth it,' came the reply (they were not wrong – Ed). Ben's manager proved equally uninterested, as were several of his friends. Then the kidnappers began ringing anybody who vaguely knew him in a desperate bid to get him off their hands. Last we heard the price had dropped to 50p and negotiations had begun with Curiosity's fan club for a whip round to rescue him.

FIVE Years
on the UK
Singles Chart

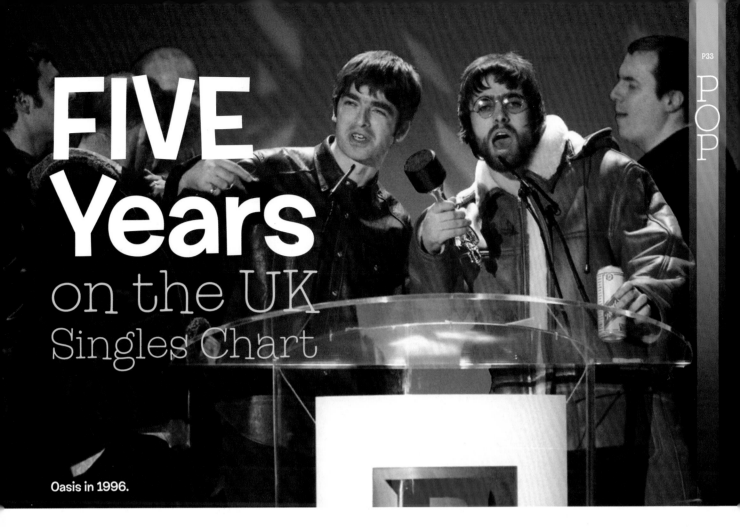

Oasis in 1996.

Bands that have spent over 260 weeks on the charts are a rare breed – some you'll find quite surprising...

The Beatles

Queen

Status Quo

Rolling Stones

The Shadows

The Bee Gees

Oasis

UB40

The Hollies

The Four Tops

Hot Chocolate

U2

The Beach Boys

Slade

Madness

Madness.

UB40.

The Day The **Music Died**

The 3 February 1959 was immortalised in the song American Pie by Don MacLean as "the day the music died". It was the day on which Buddy Holly, Ritchie Valens and the Big Bopper died in a plane crash in Iowa. Eight years later Joe Meek, the eccentric, and sometimes brilliant, record producer, shot himself after shooting dead his landlady at his flat in the Holloway Road.

Two years later John, George and Ringo signed a management deal with Allen Klein, while Paul opted to go with his father-in-law Lee Eastman. This was a year to the day after recording Lady Madonna, which was exactly four years after they arrived in NYC to begin their first US tour. Two years to the day after Buddy Holly died Bob Dylan recorded his first song, San Francisco Bay Blues. On the positive side a number of rock and pop people have been born on 3 February. On the same day as Buddy died Lol Tolhurst of the Cure was born. In 1947 Dave Davies of the Kinks and Melanie were born. A year later Ozzy – although his mum called him John – Osbourne let out his first wail. . .we'll refrain from making the obvious link.

The Name Game

Why would anyone change their name? Well check this lot out and it's not difficult to see why. Although to be fair, Brian Eno's is not really a name change, it's just reducing his name from a paragraph to just two words or sometimes one.

Adam Ant – Stuart Leslie Goddard

Captain Beefheart – Don Van Vliet

Jon Bon Jovi – John Francis Bongiovi Jr.

Bono – Paul David Hewson

David Bowie – David Robert Hayward Stenton Jones

Cher – Cherilyn Sarkisian La Piere

Eric Clapton – Eric Patrick Clapp

Alice Cooper – Vincent Damon Furnier

Elvis Costello – Declan Patrick McManus

John Denver – John Henry Deutschendorf

Bo Diddley – Otha Elias Bates McDaniel

Bob Dylan – Robert Zimmerman

Eminem – Marshall Bruce Mathers III

David Essex – David Albert Cook

Billy Idol – William Michael Albert Broad

Brian Eno – Brian Peter George St. John le Baptiste de la Salle Eno

k.d. lang – Katherine Dawn Lang

Taj Mahal – Henry St.Clair Fredericks

Meat Loaf – Marvin Lee Aday

Freddie Mercury – Frederick Farookh Bulsara

George Micheal – Yorgos Panayiotou

Notorious B.I.G. – Christopher Wallace

Cliff Richard – Harry Webb

Seal – Henry Olusegun Olumide Samuel

Dusty Springfield – Mary O'Brien

Sting – Gordon Matthew Sumner

Donna Summer – LaDonna Andrea Gaines

Tina Turner – Annie Mae Bullock

Sid Vicious – John Simon Ritchie

Stevie Wonder – Steveland Morris

John Francis Bongiovi Jr.

Steveland Morris.

Marshall Bruce Mathers III.

Henry Olusegun Olumide Samuel.

The Diary of a US TOUR

During February and March 1975 Rod Stewart and The Faces were on the penultimate tour of America. Soon Ronnie Wood would join the Stones on a full time basis and Rod would embark on his all-conquering solo career. This unique set of behind the scenes photographs shot by a Daily Mirror photographer are a wonderful insight into how touring used to be. . .

Gary Glitter and David Bowie watch from side stage.

On stage at the San Francisco Cow Palace.

Kenney Jones who later played with The Who after Keith Moon died.

Bass player Tetsu.

Backstage at the Cow Palace: Ian McLagan, Tetsu Yamauchi, Kenney Jones, Ronnie Wood and Rod Stewart.

THE EXTRAORDINARY CASE

Woody goes shopping.

Rod the Mod.

My Way

Frank meets Bobby Moore in 1971 while My Way is on its sixth go round on the British charts.

The song that has spent longer on the UK singles chart than any other – an amazing 124 weeks, that's almost twice as long as its nearest rival, which you might be surprised to know is Amazing Grace by Judy Collins. Frank Sinatra's anthem is unlikely ever to be caught with the changing world of downloads and a shift away from the single as a concept.

Besides being a karaoke classic My Way has been recorded by a whole mass of artists. It made the US charts in 1970, having been covered by Brook Benton, and again in 1977 when it got to No. 22, it being the first Elvis Presley release after his death. In Britain the Sex Pistols took it to No. 7 in 1978; almost twenty years later Shane MacGowan, the lead singer of Irish band The Pogues briefly made the Top 30. As proof of his despotic dictatorship, Saddam Hussein chose Frank's version of My Way as the theme song for his fifty-fourth birthday.

A couple of years ago it went from being My Way to the wrong way when a 25-year-old Filipino man was stabbed to death for singing it out of tune during a birthday party. Police officer Noel Albis said the victim, Casimiro Lagugad, was asked to sing Sinatra's popular song My Way during the party in Manila. Witnesses said the suspect, Julio Tugas, forty-eight, one of the guests and a neighbour of the victim, got irked because Lagugad was singing out of tune, Officer Albis said. 'Tugas suddenly attacked the victim and stabbed him in the neck,' he added. Guests rushed Mr. Lagugad to the hospital, but he died while being treated. Tugas surrendered and was later charged with homicide.

I need a HIT

According to the press release sent out with this photograph. Jonathan King posed with 17-year-old model Mary Colinson from Malta for a pin-up photograph for a calendar to be sent to disc jockeys and producers to plug his current record Let It All Hang Out that had just entered the best sellers. The message on the calendar will read – Let it all hangout for 1970.

Mr King had last had a hit in 1965 with Everyone's Gone To The Moon and this latest single staggered to No. 26 in the charts so the calendar didn't do much good. Throughout the Seventies the multi-talented pop maestro, as he was once described, continued to release a string of singles under various pseudonyms, which included Shag and Father Abraphart and the Smurfs; he also produced early recordings by The Bay City Rollers. In 2001 King went to prison having been found guilty of indecent assault and other sexual offences. It's tarnished the reputation of a man who without doubt had a prodigious talent for pop.

Sophie Ellis Bextor.

Janet Jackson.

Pink.

Natalie Imbruglia.

DIVAs

Are they all Divas, or in some cases are they just wannabe's? What makes a Diva? Is it attitude, the voice, striking the pose?

Christina Aguilera.

Dido.

Lily Allen.

Mariah Carey.

Janis Joplin.

Dusty Springfield.

Whitney Houston.

Britney Spears.

Cilla Black.

Kim Wilde.

Donna Summer.

Kate Bush.

Watched by their manager Brian Epstein in June 1963, The Beatles, John Lennon, Paul McCartney, Ringo Starr and George Harrison; Gerry and the Pacemakers: Gerry Marsden, Freddie Marsden, Les Chadwick and Les McGuire; Brian Epstein and Billy J Kramer and the Dakotas: Robin McDonald, Mike Maxfield, Billy J Kramer, Ray Jones and Tony Mansfield, all do what pop stars do best... jump!

The Sixties Quiz

If you can remember the Sixties you weren't really there! – So good luck!

1. In the Sixties a singer became the oldest person ever to have a British No. 1, what was their name?

2. The youngest female singer to ever have a British No. 1 did so in 1961; she was 14 years and 10 months, what was her name?

3. During the Sixties the EP was a big seller. The Beatles, The Shadows, Elvis, Cliff and The Rolling Stones were five of the most successful artists on the Extended Play chart with multiple No. 1s, who was the sixth?

4. Two artists had posthumous No. 1s in the Sixties; Jim Reeves was one, who was the other?

5. Which artists released an album in 1966 which has gone on to spend over two years on the UK album chart without ever having made it into the UK Top Ten?

6. In the USA The Beatles were the most successful chart band and Elvis was the most successful male, but who was the most successful female singer?

7. Bob Dylan had No. 1 hit singles in Britain and America during the Sixties – true or false?

8. Who had the most hit singles in the USA during the decade – The Four Tops or The Temptations?

9. What do Solomon Burke, Joe Tex and Barry McGuire, who all had their biggest hits in the Sixties, have in common?

10. The Beatles had six consecutive No. 1 US hit singles, but so did another group, who are they?

For the answers see page 208 where you'll also find the names of the performers pictured here.

From the Archives

According to the picture caption these are 'Young mods with hands clasped behind their backs dancing The Blues to the music of The Dave Clark Five at Basildon, Essex.' The picture dates from September 1963 as the band's first minor hit – Do You Love Me – was released; it managed to get to No. 30 in the charts and two months later the follow-up, Glad all Over came out. This single made No. 1 in January, knocking The Beatles off the top spot. It was the beginning of a roller coaster year when the DC5 were at the forefront of the 'British Invasion' of America.

Dave Clark in the centre and five nice boys.

Then & Later On
Cher

Cher, along with Sonny, burst onto the scene in the summer of 1965 with the classic I Got You Babe the 19-year-old Cher from El Centro, California had met 30-year-old Sonny while he was working for Phil Spector – they soon married. If you had asked Cher back then how long her career would last she would scarcely have believed how long it's gone on. Thirty-three years later she was back at the top of the charts with Believe – she was still looking pretty good...

Before *they were* Famous

Victoria Adams/Spice/Posh/Beckham

At seventeen Victoria Adams attended Laine Theatre Arts School in Epsom and afterwards was briefly in a band named Persuasion. Oh how very different it all might have been...

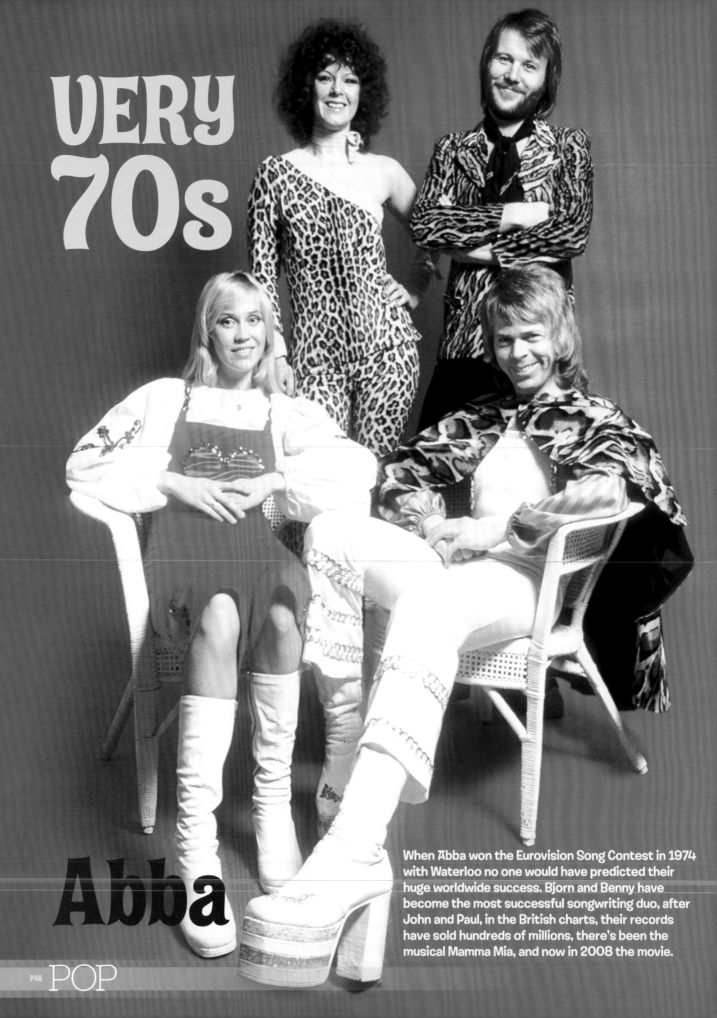

VERY 70s

Abba

When Abba won the Eurovision Song Contest in 1974 with Waterloo no one would have predicted their huge worldwide success. Bjorn and Benny have become the most successful songwriting duo, after John and Paul, in the British charts, their records have sold hundreds of millions, there's been the musical Mamma Mia, and now in 2008 the movie.

From *the* Archives

Mike Batt is now the man behind Katie Melua's success.

Elizabeth Beresford, the creator of the Wombles, with one of her characters.

According to the press handout 'Wendy, the wife of Womble king Mike Batt has gone into competition with her husband. Wendy is manager of top group Mad Hatters, a very well known disco rock group. Wendy is the only woman top group manager. Ex school teacher Wendy has two daughters. Wendy's group has a single released next week called Love Potion Number Nine, a disco rock number, which is in fierce competition with Mike Batt and the Wombles' single called The Rain Maker.'

So fierce was the competition that neither single managed to chart. The Wombles' bubble, if you can call it that, had long since burst – but four Top 10 singles and three Top 20 albums is no mean feat for a bunch of musicians dressed as kid's TV characters.

The seven ages of
Macca

Pop Star – Paul and John in 1964.

Serious Musician – February 1967, Paul with his new moustache.

Family Man – 1975 Paul, Linda and daughter Heather.

Concerned Citizen – 1985 with Bono at Live Aid.

Elder Statesman – January 1999.

Lucky in Love – July 2001 announcing his engagement to Heather Mills.

Unlucky in Love – 2008 at the Royal Courts of Justice over his divorce from Heather Mills.

David Bowie arrives at Victoria Station in May 1976 and adopts a pose redolent of a great dictator or an exiled King of Nowhere. Bowie had recently adopted a new persona, that of the 'Thin White Duke' and was on tour playing six nights at the Empire Pool Wembley.

Before *they were* Famous

Kiki Dee

Kiki Dee with a man dressed as Cupid in Piccadilly Circus for a charity event.

Kiki in 1995.

KIKI DEE KICKS IN

A FEW weeks ago she was Miss Pauline Matthews, of Bradford, Yorks.

But one disc can change all that. She is now Kiki Dee, of Discland... kicking in with a new name.

Kiki is sixteen. She has been singing in dance halls since she was thirteen. Fontana Records now launch her on her new career with a British song called "Early Night."

Miss Dee's first disc makes an infectious sound that should fall pleasantly on the teen ear.

When Elton John started his own record label in the early Seventies one of his first signings was Kiki Dee and when she had a first hit in 1973 with Amoureuse most people assumed that she'd just appeared on the scene. Nothing could have been further from the truth. As this above cutting shows Kiki had been around for quite a while and while her name was far from a household one she was well known in the music business. She'd had hits on the Northern Soul circuit, been briefly signed to Tamla Motown in 1970 and even appeared on the Benny Hill Show. Her biggest hit came in 1976 when she recorded Don't Go Breaking My Heart with Elton – it topped the charts on both sides of the Atlantic. Kiki is still performing and still in great voice.

It'll never be a HIT

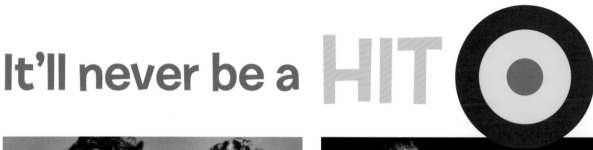

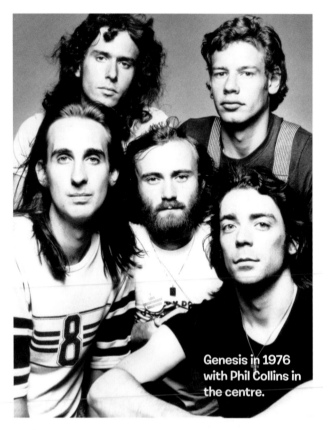

Genesis in 1976 with Phil Collins in the centre.

Mark Knopfler in 1985.

Reviewers in some respects have a thankless task for they have to pronounce on things before the rest of us get to hear them and tell us if they're going to be a hit or not. If a band is established, while they might not like a particular recording, they probably have a pretty shrewd idea of how well it will do. Not so for new acts – here are some crackers...

According to Allan Jones, the then assistant Editor of the Melody Maker, this record was 'dull, not daring and quickly unlistenable.' Having already pinned his colours to the wall by saying, 'This ridiculous epic is so comprehensively awful and clumsily pretentious that it's positively awe inspiring.' The record was Dire Straits' single, Private Investigations. While Allan didn't say whether he thought it would be a hit or not he clearly felt it didn't deserve to be. In fact it made No. 2 on the charts, the highest position any Dire Straits single would ever achieve. The Love Over Gold album from which it was taken made No. 1 in the UK and spent 200 weeks on the album charts. Mind you, Allan may just have been having a bad day because in the same issue he declared that Culture Club's Do You Really Want to Hurt Me was 'woefully ordinary.' He claimed Boy George 'sang with all the camped up theatrical galumph of Kathy Kirby.' It became the band's first No. 1 in the UK and narrowly missed the top in America staying at No. 2 for three weeks.

In May 1972 a young reporter on the South Wales Echo was given the job of reviewing the new Stones album, Exile On Main Street. 'The Rolling Stones have a talent for survival. They've been a monster success for almost a decade. But I've an awful feeling it won't last much longer. With their new double album they seem to have reached a dead end.' His name was Ken Follett, six years before his eleventh novel, The Eye Of The Needle, became a best seller.

'Noisy drumming marks the introduction. I wonder who it is making that flaming row – probably a flaming youth.' So began a review of Flaming Youth's single, Man Woman and Child in July 1970. Within the month Youth's drummer had quit and beaten fourteen others to join aspiring legends, Genesis. The drummer's name? Phil Collins of course.

From *the* **Archives**

Led Zeppelin

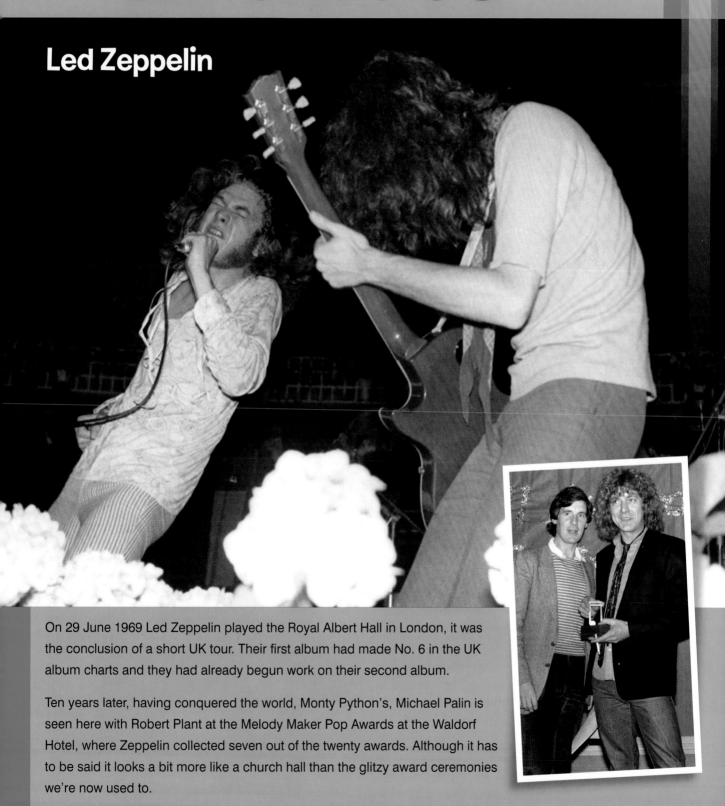

On 29 June 1969 Led Zeppelin played the Royal Albert Hall in London, it was the conclusion of a short UK tour. Their first album had made No. 6 in the UK album charts and they had already begun work on their second album.

Ten years later, having conquered the world, Monty Python's, Michael Palin is seen here with Robert Plant at the Melody Maker Pop Awards at the Waldorf Hotel, where Zeppelin collected seven out of the twenty awards. Although it has to be said it looks a bit more like a church hall than the glitzy award ceremonies we're now used to.

Anything
for
FAME

The fickle finger of fame can point in your direction or it can just as easily stop pointing your way. In order to achieve fame bands will do anything – well almost anything. But when they start sliding down the greasy snake to oblivion there's absolutely nothing they won't do to stop their decline and fall.

Joe Dolce is a genuine one-hit wonder. His Shaddap You Face was the only recording of his ever to chart and it made No. 1. Released under the name of the Joe Dolce Music Theatre in 1981 he was a 34-year-old American born guy who lived in Australia. He has a lot to answer for because it kept Ultravox's Vienna from the top of the charts.

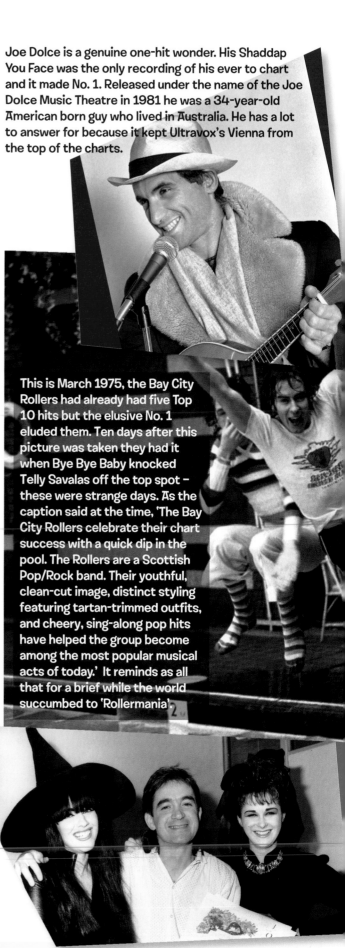

This is March 1975, the Bay City Rollers had already had five Top 10 hits but the elusive No. 1 eluded them. Ten days after this picture was taken they had it when Bye Bye Baby knocked Telly Savalas off the top spot – these were strange days. As the caption said at the time, 'The Bay City Rollers celebrate their chart success with a quick dip in the pool. The Rollers are a Scottish Pop/Rock band. Their youthful, clean-cut image, distinct styling featuring tartan-trimmed outfits, and cheery, sing-along pop hits have helped the group become among the most popular musical acts of today.' It reminds as all that for a brief while the world succumbed to 'Rollermania'.

When Strawberry Switchblade did this photo shoot in July 1983 they were still dreaming of chart success. It would be another sixteen months before they finally tasted fame when their single, Since Yesterday, made the Top 10 in Britain. It was short-lived though, because the next two singles couldn't even get into the Top 50 despite this radical change of image.

Back in 1974 everyone was Kung Fu Fighting according to Carl Douglas, and it went to No. 1; from then on it was steadily downhill and nothing else he did even made the Top 20.

In July 1971 Edison Lighthouse released their new record Hawaiian Island according to their press handout. It must have been so bad because no one seems to be able to remember it and it certainly didn't trouble the charts. The original Edison Lighthouse who had a hit with Love Grows Where My Rosemary Goes was a studio band based around session singer Tony Burrows; this version of the band was hastily assembled to plug the gap after Burrows and the others involved in that hit went their own way. Still these lads probably had some fun during their brief period almost in the spotlight.

In April 1976 Sailor were promoting their single Girls, Girls, Girls which made No. 7 in the UK charts. From left to right, back row: Anne-Marie, George Kajanus, Kay Leary and Grant Serpell. Front; Jilly Johnson, Henry Marsh, Phil Pickett and Linda Bran. The models were not in the group, but were just there to make the point. Later Jilly Johnson did form Blonde on Blonde, with another model, Nina Carter – they didn't have a hit.

PR people think of the most bizarre ideas for a photo shoot. Here's The Kaiser Chiefs in Armstrong's in Edinburgh's Grassmarket to buy themselves some clothes for their Scottish gigs they were about to play in April 2005. To be fair their first album had just come out but even so! Left to right there's Peanut, Andrew White, Ricky Wilson, Nick Hodgson, and Simon Rix.

Simple Minds in 1984.

If you can hum these, then you're
A HUGE Fan

Everyone has to start somewhere and not everyone is an overnight sensation. These are all records that failed to make any real dent on the charts by bands that would go on to be very big.

Never Gonna Cry Again - The Eurythmics (No. 63 in 1981)

Running Free - Iron Maiden (No. 34 in 1980)

Who Needs Love Like That - Erasure (No. 55 in 1985)

Holiday 80 - The Human League (No. 56 in 1980)

Dreaming Of Me - Depeche Mode (No. 57 in 1981)

In the City - The Jam (No. 40 in 1977)

I Wanna Be Your Lover – Prince (No. 41 in 1980)

Kings Of The Wild Frontier - Adam Ant (No. 48 in 1980)

Life In A Day - Simple Minds (No. 62 in 1979)

Red Frame, White Light - OMD (No. 67 in 1980)

Promises - Take That (No. 38 in 1991)

She's So High - Blur (No. 48 in 1990)

Lip Gloss - Pulp (No. 50 - 1993)

Damon Albarn of Blur.

Phil Oakey and Joanne Catherall of Human League.

It's very HEAVY man

Back in 1983 former member of Deep Purple Ian Gillan was taking a break from singing about smoke on the water to lend his vocal talents to Black Sabbath. Their former lead singer, and reality TV show host, John 'Ozzy' Osbourne had left four years earlier, mumbling about musical differences, to front his own band, Blizzard of Oz. Ian and Black Sabbath had recorded a new album which they were inspired to call, Born Again. The album cover featured a baby painted red with two little yellow fangs as well as rather fetching yellow painted finger nails – is it any wonder heavy metal causes the odd raised eyebrow? The band planned to tour North America on the strength of their new album and called a meeting to discuss the stage set, always central to any rock bands, live show. In another piece of inspired thinking bass player Geezer Butler suggested that a life-size model of Stonehenge be built and then erected on stage from where the Sabs could entertain their vast legion of fans with some of their new material. Among the tracks on Born Again is a one minute fifty-eight second, far from classic, song entitled Stonehenge, along with Digital Bitch, Zero the Hero and the obligatory title track. It all added up to what is widely regarded as the band's creative nadir.

Thoughts of nadirs, creative or otherwise, were the farthest things from the band's collective consciousness. Week long rehearsals were arranged at the Maple Leaf hockey stadium in Montreal where the henge set was erected and the band went through their paces. As the week was drawing to a close a dwarf turned up and was promptly dressed in a red leotard and given little yellow fangs to cap his teeth. At the final day's dress rehearsal the dwarf was placed astride the highest stone and as the music reached a crescendo a pre-recorded scream rang out and the dwarf fell backwards off the henge onto a pile of mattresses that were discreetly placed out of sight of where the audience were to sit. At which point bells start tolling, roadies dressed as monks start crawling across the front of the stage and the wistful tones of Sabbath's 1970 classic (?) War Pigs began........................"Hello, MONTREAL!"

Black Sabbath from the left Terry 'Geezer' Butler Tony Lommi, Bev Bevan and Ian Gillan.

Then & Later On
Take That

Robbie Williams, Jason Orange, Mark Owen, Gary Barlow and Howard Donald on 10 October 1992, the day that A Million Love Songs entered the UK charts, the turning point for the band on their way to becoming the biggest British boy band of all time. Like all bands they were not averse to a bit of leaping in the air.

In 2006 the boy band became a man band, playing a hugely successful tour in arenas and stadiums. The year culminated in their album, Beautiful World going multi-platinum driven by their great single Patience.

Messin' with Mahesh

From left to right: Denis Wilson, Al Jardine, Mike Love, The Maharishi, Bruce Johnston and Carl Wilson.

To say for definite what was the most unsuccessful tour of all time is perhaps difficult, as the criteria could be open to some debate. But certainly The Beach Boys US tour in May 1968 would probably win the award for the least successful tour by a major band. While admittedly the band's fortunes had slipped slightly since the heady days of December 1966 when Good Vibrations went to No. 1 in America they were still very popular. The band had become involved with the Maharishi Mahesh Yogi, particularly so after Mike Love visited India in early 1968 along with The Beatles. After Mike returned he wrote and the band recorded Transcendental Meditation in April. A tour of seventeen cities was organised, with the Maharishi as The Beach boys 'opening act'. Unfortunately anyone who bothered to attend the gigs quickly got bored with what the great man had to say while seated on a stage surrounded by masses of flowers. According to Bruce Johnston, 'Even the funeral in The Godfather had fewer flowers.' Catcalls are said to have drowned out much of his teachings. Pretty soon the MMY found he had a better offer, a movie contract, and he jumped ship and The Beach Boys cancelled the rest of the shows.

According to Al Jardine, "if anybody benefits from this tour it will be florists." In fact The Beach Boys are said to have lost around $500,000, somewhere between $5-6 million today. It in fact marked a turning point in their career, as shortly after the tour their new album, Friends (which included Transcendental Meditation) could only stagger to No. 126 in the Billboard chart. While it did make No. 13 in Britain things for the band in America were never quite the same. It would be another eight years before they again had an American Top 10 single.

Stars and their Pets!

Pop stars are pet lovers too...

Somehow you just know these dogs belong to Elton John. Left is Dennis and right is Joseph. Named after who we wonder?

Roger Daltrey of The Who and his nine-month-old Salouki named Mouse at the singer's flat in St Johns Wood, London in September 1966. The Who were at No. 2 with I'm A Boy.

Just the sort of dog that Ozzy would have don't you think? At home in 1998.

Sandie Shaw with her pet dog in January 1969, around the time of her Monsieur Dupont, last Top 10 hit.

Ringo and his wife Barbara with their dogs in 1981; we're unable to confirm whether they're called John and Paul.

Paul and Linda McCartney with their dog Ringo at their farm near Campbeltown in Scotland in 1971.

We're not sure that Seagulls count as pets but nevertheless this is Billy Fury in 1977 with two gulls. Billy, one of the truly great British rock and rollers died in 1983 aged just forty-two.

Geri Halliwell in 1999 with her dog Harry.

Sting with his dog in 1986.

The 80s
Revisited

Sheena Easton

Sheena photographed at Glasgow Airport in March 1980 as Modern Girl, her first single was released; it made No. 56. Its success in part came from being featured on a BBC reality TV show, what seems strange, given the world that we now live in, is that it didn't do better. However the follow-up 9 to 5 or Morning Train as it was called in the US made No. 3 in Britain. It topped the US charts and kick started her career in the US where she was far more successful than in Britain. In the Eighties six more of her singles made the US Top 10, while just two did similarly in the UK. She lives in America these days and has been a regular performer in Las Vegas, not bad for a girl from Bellshill in North Lanarkshire, Scotland.

Bob Dylan and Joan Baez in the Savoy Gardens on the Thames embankment in April 1965. Dylan's first British hit, The Times They Are A-Changin' had just entered the charts. His UK concerts were the last time he played entirely acoustic shows; it also marked the end of his relationship with Joan Baez.

Not so very Great Moments in Rock

No. 49

On 30 May 1975 Rick Wakeman and the cast of what seemed like thousands were photographed at Wembley. This was a time when Rick was one of the biggest things in rock music and to prove it he staged his over the top live performance of The Myths And Legends of King Arthur and The Knights of the Round Table. It featured a full orchestra and naturally enough ice skaters! This show helped redefine pomp rock and in so doing set in train much of what we now take for granted in live shows, although it's not stopped just about everyone from sticking the boot into poor old Rick. Whatever the shows merits, it cost him a huge amount of money, and the audience got to hear lyrics such as 'Gone are the days of the Knights, of the Round Table and fights.' It probably gives you some idea of what it was all about.

Then & Later On
Iggy Pop

February 1977.

Iggy Pop and the Stooges on the main stage at the Isle of Wight music festival – 14 June 2008 – just thirty-one years on.

The seven ages of Michael Jackson

Brotherly Love – The Jackson Five, although the eagle-eyed among you will spot the fact that there's six. In front is little brother Randy who joined the group four years later.

Solo Star – 1979.

Superstar in waiting –1984.

Superstar – In concert at Cardiff Arms Park in 1988.

Married Man – 1994 Michael Jackson and Lisa Marie Presley arrive in Hungary.

No Direction Home – 1997.

Lost – Michael Jackson at Harrods with his good friend Mohammad Al Fayed.

The real Prince of Wales?

A NEW GROUP from Wales look like giving the Liverpool lads something to think about. Tom Jones and the Playboys make their disc debut with Chills and Fever (Decca), and it's great shakes.

This clip from the Daily Mirror announcing Tom's arrival on the scene proved a little premature, although it certainly proved to be true. Tom's first hit, It's Not Unusual which came out in February 1965, was at No. 1 by March, and while it wasn't a Liverpool band he knocked off the top of the charts it was the start of what has been a long and glorious career. His second No. 1 knocked The Beach Boys from the top of the UK singles charts in December 1966.

From the Archives

Jimi Hendrix

Journalist Godfrey Winn in December 1967, rehearsing for the Good Evening programme at ATV Studios in Elstree with Jimi Hendrix, Noel Redding and Mitch Mitchell. No wonder Jimi's looking a little perplexed because the indefatigable Mr Winn, who had recently written his autobiography, had recorded a single, which according to the paper was 'self confessedly for squares rather than swingers.'

The record was called I Pass and had Winn speaking the lyrics over a ballad-style backing track. It wasn't a hit. Jimi and the Experience performed Spanish Castle Magic, the only time he ever performed the album track from Axis Bold As Love on television.

The Summer of LOVE

Musically 1967 was the year the world changed forever. The year began with Tom Jones at the top of the charts singing about the Green Green Grass of Home and ended with John, Paul, George and Ringo singing Hello Goodbye.

It was when Jimi Hendrix arrived on the scene and, The Beach Boys turned from 'Heroes to Villains'. Somehow amid the beads, kaftans and droopy moustaches Engelbert Humperdinck managed to top the charts with Release Me preventing The Beatles Penny Lane/Strawberry Fields Forever from making No. 1. The Hippy phenomenon was everywhere – even the Troggs sang that Love is All Around and the Stones were anxious to Let's Spend The Night Together.

Surrounded by all the love, peace and happiness Mick Jagger and Keith Richards were trying to avoid a jail sentence and in the process they turned pop from the sole preserve of the music press to tabloid news. But it was also a year in which The Beatles were nominated for eight Grammies, and won just two: beaten twice by Frank Sinatra, and once by The New Vaudeville Band's Winchester Cathedral.

And there's the Vietnam War; Sandie Shaw won the Eurovision song contest; Frank Zappa and the Mothers of Invention tour the UK for the first time; Elvis got married; Carl Wilson of The Beach Boys was charged with draft dodging; the Monterey Pop Festival is held and becomes the template for hundreds more over the coming decades; Jimi Hendrix was a support act for The Monkees on their UK tour (he quit after just seven dates!); the Pirate Radio stations stop broadcasting; BBC Radio 1 starts broadcasting; 'A Whiter Shade of Pale' tops the charts; The Beatles embark upon a Magical Mystery Tour; Otis Redding died in a plane crash, and the Shadows were still Britain's favourite instrumental group. The release of Sergeant Peppers Lonely Hearts Club Band – what more could anyone ask for?

Keith Richards and Mick Jagger on their way to court.

John Lennon, Ringo Starr and George Harrison at Bangor on 27 August, on their way to see the Maharishi.

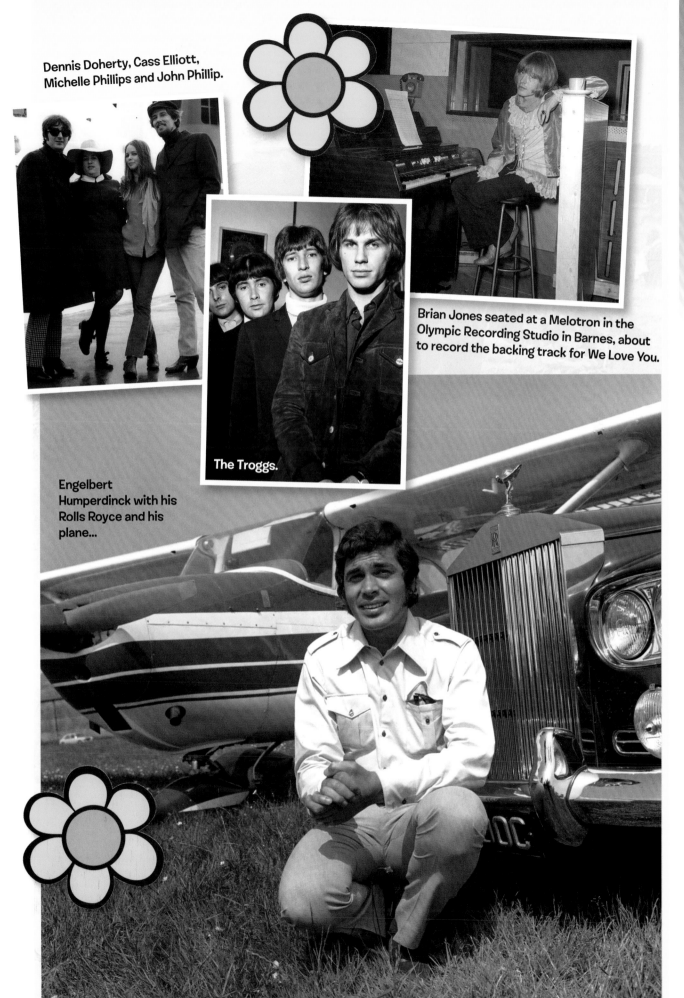

Dennis Doherty, Cass Elliott, Michelle Phillips and John Phillip.

The Troggs.

Brian Jones seated at a Melotron in the Olympic Recording Studio in Barnes, about to record the backing track for We Love You.

Engelbert Humperdinck with his Rolls Royce and his plane...

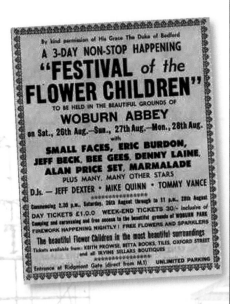

POP Fesivals

Many think that Woodstock was the first 'pop festival' but prior to 1969 there had been many such gatherings of music lovers in both the USA and the UK. In America the Newport Festival was probably the inspiration for the Richmond Jazz & Blues Festival. After Woodstock it seemed like there was a festival every week! There was Bath, the Isle of Wight, Bickershaw and a whole host more.

The line-up at the 1969 Isle of Wight Festival, it's amazing how many of those acts are still performing forty years on.

View of the main stage at the 10th International Jazz & Blues Festival, Plumpton Race Course, Sussex in August 1970. All very civilised with chairs to sit on!

Keanu Reeves with his group, Dogstar, on stage in the NME Tent at T in the Park.

T in the Park at Strathclyde Park in 1995.

Glittering **Glastonbury**

Everyone wants to play the Glastonbury Music Festival – Amy Winehouse on the Pyramid stage in 2008, Neil Diamond (2008), Duffy (2008), Pete Doherty (2007), Chris Martin of Coldplay (2005) and finally Rolf Harris in 2002.

Then & Later On
Midge Ure

How do you start out in a glam, boy band, then record one of the Eighties classic anthems, before going on to save the planet? Well ask Midge Ure, a lad from Cambuslang in Lanarkshire, with more than his fair share of dreams. Having flirted with pop in Glasgow Midge moved onto punk and nearly became a member of the Sex Pistols. He and Bob Geldof founded Live Aid and Midge is still a member of the Band Aid Trust. Seeing Midge perform Vienna, Ultravox's biggest hit, today and it's like turning the clock back. He's a bigger talent than the acclaim he's received.

Slik in 1977.

Midge in classical mode.

Before *they were* Famous

Queen

In December 1973 Queen posed for this picture close by to EMI, their label's London office. It was to support the release of their first single, Keep Yourself Alive, which failed to chart and really gave little indication of what they would become. Freddie's sense of style and flamboyance is there for all to see – even John Deacon looks stylish! A year later and Killer Queen had gone to No. 2 in the UK – a new rock dynasty had been established. By late 1975 Bohemian Rhapsody was topping the charts – despite some people at their record label thinking it was too long to be a single and should have been edited.

THE WHO
Live at Charlton
31st May 1974

In front of 65,000 fans, including 5,000 gatecrashers at Charlton Athletic's stadium, the Valley, The Who were supported by the Alex Harvey Band, Little Feat, the Outlaws, and Streetwalkers.

Paul McCartney and Linda saying hello to Princess Diana after their show in Lille, France in November 1992.

Prince William, Natasha Bedingfield, Tom Jones, Joss Stone and Prince Harry at Wembley Stadium, for the concert in memory of Diana, Princess of Wales.

Pop go the Royals

There's always been something slightly incongruous about royalty mixing with pop stars, although at least Prince William and Prince Harry have followed in their Mother's footsteps – they know who they're talking to.

Princess Diana and Michael Jackson in July 1988.

... gham Palace in June 2002. Prince William with Tom Jones, Shirley Bassey and Ozzy Osbourne. These 'royal' pop events always create the most odd collection of artists.

The Queen meets Ozzy Osbourne... the mind boggles.

Prince Charles meets the Corrs at the Party in the Park concert for the Prince's Trust in July 2000. 'One thought you were awfully good.'

Champagne performed at Prince Charles' 31st birthday party in November 1979. I guess it's not rude to point if you're royalty.

The Three Degrees meet Prince Charles after a charity show at a Country Club in Eastbourne, Sussex, July 1978. "Now you're what one calls a popular music group."

Prince Charles gets a rib tickler when he meets All Saints at the Party in the Park for the Prince's Trust Concert in July 1998. 'One thought you were awfully good too.'

Pop Stars Go Topless

In the best traditions of providing our readers with the kind of pictures you just love, we bring you...

Steve Harley in 1975, lead singer with Cockney Rebel and now a Radio 2 DJ.

Spandau Ballet in November 1982 recording their new album in the Bahamas. Tony Hadley, Steve Norman, Martin Kemp, John Keeble, Gary Kemp.

Adam Ant at the Palladium in Hollywood, Los Angeles; the Antman had three UK No. 1s and another seven Top 10 hits which might well surprise you.

AC/DC, twenty-eight UK hits and not one of them ever made the Top 10.

Freddie Mercury, never one to hold back.

American punk band, The Tubes in 1978.

Prince at Wembley in 1986, obviously a good year for going topless.

Bobby Brown in 1995.

Lux Interior, singer with The Cramps in 1986.

Daniel O'Donnell, one for our older lady readers.

Well, she did have a couple of hits!

VERY 70s

Cast your mind back to a time long ago, when the Open University began, Rolls Royce went bankrupt, Evel Knievel set a world record by jumping over 19 cars, some of Charles Manson's followers were sentenced to the gas chamber, the UK opted out of the space race, Disney World opens in Florida, Intel releases the first microprocessor and Slade had their first hit record. It is of course 1971 and that's when Get Down and Get With It stormed up the charts to No. 16.

Slade

For the next three years Slade were enormous, twelve Top 10 hit records in Britain, half of them going to No. 1. They never could break through in America where their biggest hit only made No. 20 and that was in 1984, when they were well past their prime. Left to right they are Dave Hill, Don Powell, Jimmy Lea and Noddy Holder.

The Seventies Quiz

1. What links Barry Manilow and Bruce Johnston of the Beach Boys?

2. Two British solo singers were the most successful on the US charts during the decade, who were they?

3. The first four Jackson 5 singles topped the US charts, true or false?

4. How many singles by The Jackson 5 and The Jacksons topped the UK charts?

5. T. Rex had four UK No. 1 singles in 1971 & '72, can you name them?

6. In 1972 who was the youngest singer ever to top the UK singles chart?

7. In 1975 an artist became the oldest ever to top the UK album charts, what was his name?

8. David Bowie topped the UK singles chart in the Seventies, true or false?

9. How many times did The Beatles top the UK singles chart during the decade?

10. How many times did The Rolling Stones top the UK singles chart in the Seventies?

For the answers see page 208.

Rolling Stones in 1971.

The Jacksons.

Bruce Johnston.

Marc Bolan of T.Rex.

PUNK

If 1967 was 'The Summer of Love' then 1977 was 'The Year of Punk', although for a few years any new group that looked a bit scruffy was called a punk band. Today magazines and radio programmes wax lyrical about how punk dominated the scene in that year, but like is so often the case things were not quite as they seem. In 1977 David Soul was huge, so were Abba of course, and Macca's Mull of Kintyre started its nine-week run at No. 1. It was also the year that Elvis died and his first posthumous release, Way Down, spent five weeks at No. 1. Nevertheless, Punk provided the newspapers with just the sort of thing their readers love to hate. Boys spitting, swearing on TV, no respect for anyone, especially their elders, and they looked very dirty – it all made The Rolling Stones look respectable.

The Sex Pistols in Holland in 1977.

Johnny Rotten of the Sex Pistols in December 1977, a perfectly turned out punk.

Sid Vicious, bass player with the Sex Pistols, who died of a heroin overdose in 1979.

The Clash in 1980.

Siouxsie & The Banshees in 1978.

The Stranglers in 1979.

Phil Jones, of Afraid of Mice, with his girlfriend, Mandy Todd, whose nose rings are linked by a chain – I wonder what they're up to now, still linked?

Then & Later On
Mick & Keith

Mick in 1965.

Keith in June 1964 during the Stones first US Tour.

Keith and Mick on stage at Twickenham in 2006.

The Eagles.

The biggest selling albums in the world
EVER

It's been a matter of discussion, argument and civilised debate, in pubs, living rooms, bars and cars the length and breadth of Britain. We've used a whole range of resources to come up with what is probably the answer. . .but then again we might just be wrong.

108 Million – Thriller – Michael Jackson

42 Million – Back in Black – AC/DC
– The Bodyguard (Soundtrack) – Whitney Houston

41 Million – Their Greatest Hits 1971-1975 – Eagles

40 Million – Saturday Night Fever (Soundtrack) – Bee Gees
– Dark Side of the Moon –Pink Floyd

37 Million – Bat Out of Hell –Meat Loaf

36 Million – Come On Over – Shania Twain

32 Million – Sgt Pepper's Lonely Hearts Club Band – Beatles
– Falling Into You – Celine Dion
– Led Zeppelin IV – Led Zeppelin
– Music Box – Mariah Carey
– Dirty Dancing (Soundtrack)

31 Million – Let's Talk About Love – Celine Dion

30 Million – Jagged Little Pill – Alanis Morissette
– Millennium – Backstreet Boys
– No. 1s – The Beatles
– Abbey Road – The Beatles
– Spirits Having Flown – The Bee Gees
– Brothers in Arms – Dire Straits

Mr Meatloaf.

Celine Dion.

Timmy Mallet.

Ten Songs that are certain to ruin a quiet night out in Spain...

or anywhere else for that matter!

1. **Agadoo** - Black Lace
2. **Dolce Vita** - Ryan Paris
3. **Una Paloma Blanca** - Jonathan King
4. **Y Viva Espana** - Sylvia
5. **I'm Too Sexy** - Right Said Fred
6. **The Birdie Song** - The Tweets
7. **The Cheeky Song (Touch My Bum)** - The Cheeky Girls
8. **Tarzan Boy** - Baltimora
9. **Itsy Bitsy Teeny Weeny Yellow Polka Dot Bikini** - Bombalurina featuring Timmy Mallett
10. **Anything by Peter Andre**

Peter Andre.

Black Lace.

Right Said Fred.

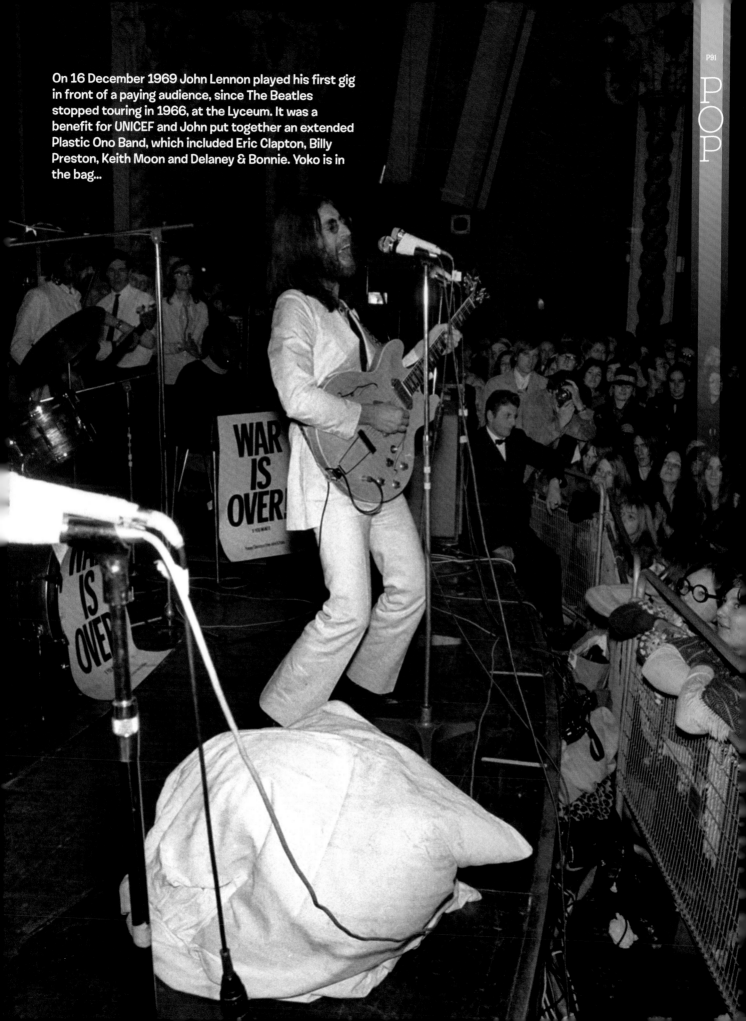

On 16 December 1969 John Lennon played his first gig in front of a paying audience, since The Beatles stopped touring in 1966, at the Lyceum. It was a benefit for UNICEF and John put together an extended Plastic Ono Band, which included Eric Clapton, Billy Preston, Keith Moon and Delaney & Bonnie. Yoko is in the bag...

Sportsmen SING

When Chris and Glenn, that's Waddle and Hoddle, stormed up the charts in 1987 the world was agog that two sportsmen could actually sing! Of course there had been recordings by various football teams in a jokey sing-a-long way, but Glenn and Chris were a genuine attempt at making a proper record. There was of course Kevin Keegan's Head Over Heels in Love back in 1979 – let's just say he was a lot better as a footballer.

It's not just footballers who like to sing a bit. Australian cricketer Don Bradman, one of the greatest batsmen of all time, fancied himself as a bit of a crooner. In 1930 Columbia Records asked him to record something, which they assumed would be a talk on cricket. The Don had other plans; he recorded two songs – Old Fashioned Locket and Our Bungalow Of Dreams. Copies are rarer than rare, but it would be interesting to hear the Don sing.

Then & Later On
Eric Clapton

In June 1967 Eric Clapton was in Cream and according to the press handout with this photograph 'Eric shows off his curly hair that is created for him by a West End ladies hairdresser.'

In June 1999 at the Launch of the Auction of Eric Clapton's guitars. He's holding a Fender Stratocaster that he bought in 1957 and played on Layla in 1972.

The 80s
Revisited

ABC

Why are ABC dressed like this? The answer can only be that it was the 80s. The band had a phenomenally successful, and very good album, The Lexicon of Love, released in the summer of 1982 it went to No. 1 spending almost a year on the charts.

Then & Later On
Johnny Rotten

John Lydon or Johnny Rotten as he was known as
in the original incarnation of the Sex Pistols was
everything a punk rocker should be. He'd
apparently acquired his pseudonym as a result of
his green teeth! As a child he had spinal meningitis,
which accounts for his trademark stare. After the
Pistols broke up he formed Public Image Limited –
PIL, who lasted fourteen years, with only modest
success. Since then he's been a Celebrity in the
Jungle, appeared on various TV projects and
currently lives in Los Angeles.

On stage at SECC
Glasgow July 1996.

The seven ages of
Rod the Mod

Rock God in Training – September 1971, with his Melody Maker Pop Award.

Pop Poseur – Rod in 1973.

Make-Up Artist – Rod and Elton John make it up back stage in December 1976.

Superstar – In January 1980 rehearsing for a tour.

Megastar – Interestingly the caption to this photo reads, 'Veteran Rocker Rod Stewart went down a storm at Wembley Stadium on 15 July 1986. Rod had an emotional reunion with his old backing band, The Faces, watched by 60,000 fans.' That was over two decades ago!

The White Stuff – Rod and Penny Lancaster in 2007 at a pre wedding party near Portofino.

ExPat – Rod in New York in 1999.

EUROVISION

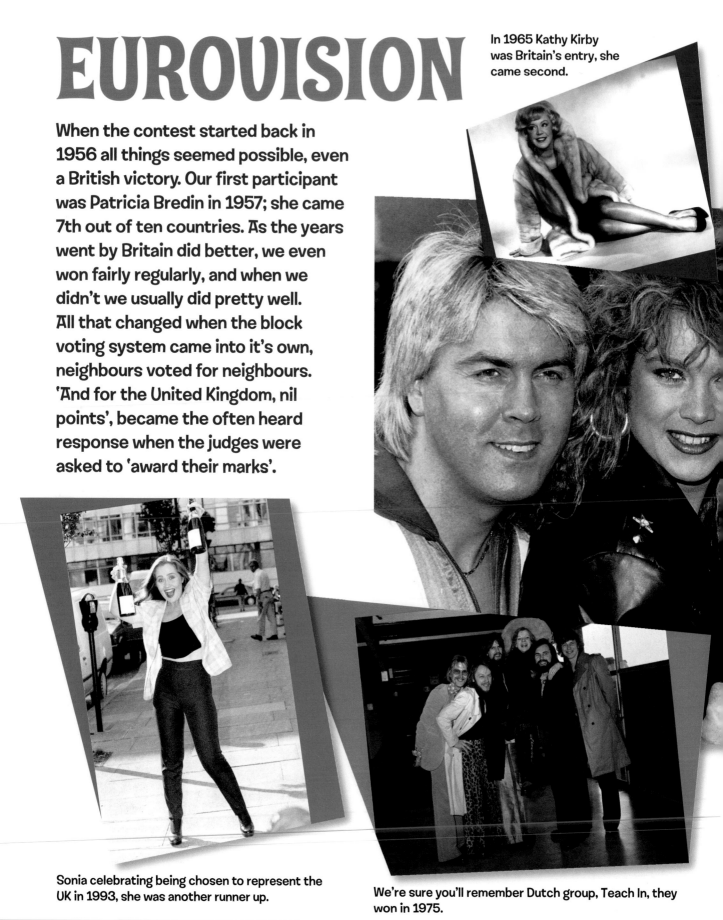

When the contest started back in 1956 all things seemed possible, even a British victory. Our first participant was Patricia Bredin in 1957; she came 7th out of ten countries. As the years went by Britain did better, we even won fairly regularly, and when we didn't we usually did pretty well. All that changed when the block voting system came into it's own, neighbours voted for neighbours. 'And for the United Kingdom, nil points', became the often heard response when the judges were asked to 'award their marks'.

In 1965 Kathy Kirby was Britain's entry, she came second.

Sonia celebrating being chosen to represent the UK in 1993, she was another runner up.

We're sure you'll remember Dutch group, Teach In, they won in 1975.

Black Lace who came 7th for Britain in 1979.

Abba in Brighton where they won the contest in 1974 with Waterloo.

Bucks Fizz won in 1981 with Making Your Mind Up. From left to right this is them in 1989, still touring – Mike Nolan, Shelly Preston, Cheryl Baker and Bobby Gee.

Clodagh Rogers, the British entrant in 1971 – she came fourth with Jack in the Box.

The Shadows at Heathrow Airport en route to Stockholm to represent Britain in 1975 – it was another second place.

Brotherhood of Man won in 1976.

Hair Today

Green is the new black – Keith Flint of The Prodigy.

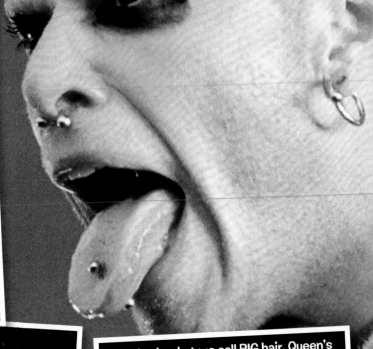

The Jesus and Mary Chain.

Mick Hucknall and Simply Red when he was little more than a lad.

Now that's what we call BIG hair, Queen's Brian May.

Kajagoogoo, their lead singer Limahl, who is in the middle at the front, is more remembered for his hair than anything he ever sang.

It's not what you got, it's how you use it – Angus Young of AC/DC.

The Cure 1986.

The hair, the hair! Geri Halliwell in 1999.

Burst who aimed to make it big in 1979 and missed.

Nearly Famous

A small tribute to all those bands that had their photographs taken, only for their records to sink without trace. Why in three out of the four bands do so many people seem keen on crouching? Perhaps that's why it didn't work out for them – they should have jumped instead. We'd love to know where are they now? All answers on a postcard...

Busker with athlete Brendan Foster (far left) and Lindisfarne's Ray Jackson on the far right.

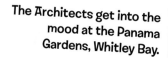

The Architects get into the mood at the Panama Gardens, Whitley Bay.

Newcastle band Buzz in 1977.

From the *Archives*

The Rolling Stones on Juke Box Jury

MICK JAGGER

CHARLIE WATTS

BRIAN JONES

KEITH RICHARD

BILL WYMAN

Mick, Charlie, Brian, Keith and Bill on 27 June 1964 rehearsing for the TV show, the first time there had ever been five panelists, there were normally only four. The BBC was expecting a record 20 million viewers for this show, instead of the usual 12 million. Filmed at Shepherds Bush Studio in London the show was compered by David Jacobs, who can still be heard on Radio 2.

On the show itself, it was very hard to get five different opinions on the records that were played to them as the band had very similar tastes in music. The BBC paid the Stones £157 10s and after it was over they had to make a dash for it as they were filming Top of the Pops later.

Nudestock

You're probably thinking don't be daft, they mean Woodstock. . .well there is just such an event, although our picture is of Queens of The Stone Age's Josh Homme getting into the true spirit of Nudestock – the only problem being it's the Reading Festival. Nudestock started in 1995 when the first annual festival took place in Michigan. Whereas at Woodstock and countless other festivals, nudity was optional, at this one it was mandatory, but fortunately not for the bands. 'We're not paid to take our clothes off,' said Alan Parsons; his Project was one of the headliners. Others on the bill included Foreigner and Kansas, and the latter's Rich Williams, who remained clothed throughout, seemed to sum up the experience for everyone. 'And you're standing there playing and there's some guy with a baseball hat and tennis shoes standing in front of you, wiggling around and playing air guitar with his pecker. It bothers you.' Lots of bum notes?

The following year the organisers were hopeful of getting Oasis (the consequences could have been mind-boggling), Blur and Supergrass to participate, but they all declined. By the 7th Nudestock in 2004 the headliners were reduced to a Beatles tribute band and Tombstone Shadow – said to be more like Creedence Clearwater Revival than the original band.

VERY 70s

Ian Dury (centre with microphone) with Robin Gibb (left of Dury), Leo Sayer (front far right), Nick Lowe (back far left), Jeff Lynne (left of Gibb) and members of the Electric Light Orchestra and The Barron Knights at the Daily Mirror 'Rock and Pop awards' at the Café Royal, London in 1979.

Frank Zappa and the Mothers of Invention in June 1970 just prior to their appearance at the Bath Pop Festival. Frank Zappa (foreground), George Duke, Ian Underwood, Jeff Simmons, Mark Volman, Howard Kalen and Aynsley Dunbar.

Clapton with Pattie Boyd in March 1975 at the premiere of the movie Tommy.

POP'S
Greatest Muse
Pattie Boyd

Pattie must hold the record for being the inspiration for the most pop songs.

I Need You - Beatles

For You Blue - Beatles

So Sad - George Harrison

Layla - Derek & The Dominoes

Wonderful Tonight - Eric Clapton

The Shape You're In - Eric Clapton

Pretty Girl - Eric Clapton

Man in love - Eric Clapton

Pattie and George Harrison in 1965.

On George Harrison's 1974 Dark Horse album he covered the Everly Brothers Bye Bye Love, a reference to his recent split from his wife Pattie. On the album credits it says Eric and Pattie Clapton are on Bye Bye Love; ironically Pattie had left George for Eric. According to George they never were on the album. 'I had to write the credits in about ten minutes as I was going on tour and I put Bye Bye Love – Pattie and Eric Clapton. The record company saw that and thought they must have appeared and typed – Eric Clapton appears courtesy of RSO Records. He hadn't appeared on it at all.

Twenty Five
Country
Music Classics

My uncle used to love me but she died
– Roger Miller

You're the reason our kids are ugly – Loretta
Lynn & Conway Twitty

The power of positive drinking – Mickey Gilley

**Drop kick me Jesus through the goalposts of
life** – Bobby Bare

**The interstate is coming through my
outhouse** – Billy Edd Wheeler

I'm gonna get a whino to decorate our house
– David Frizzell

Who wants a slightly ugly woman – Connie Cato

My can do, can't keep up with my want to
– Nat Stuckey

**My head hurts, my feet stink and I don't love
you** – Jimmy Buffett

She got the goldmine, I got the shaft
– Jerry Reed

Three sheets in the wind – Reba McEntire

This is my last hangover – Roger Harris

**I had a good woman but she married
Lawrence** – Doug Kershaw

Does anyone make love at home anymore?
– Moe Bandy

**Take this job and shove it (I ain't working here
no more)** – Johnny Paycheck

Store bought teeth – Carson Robinson

Go somewhere and find yourself a sheep
– Don Bowman

**Just dropped in to see what condition my
condition was in** – Kenny Rogers

You can't roller skate in a buffalo herd
– Roger Miller

**I'm an old lump of coal, I'll be a diamond some
day** – John Anderson

The man that turned my mama on
– Tanya Tucker

The wino and I know – Jimmy Buffett

**You cut up the clothes in the closet of our
dreams** – Joshie Jo Armstead

May the bird of paradise fly up your nose –
Little Jimmy Dickens

Don't all the girls get prettier at closing time
– Mickey Gilley

Boyband Bonanza

There's always been boybands... that's how most bands start out. It became the thing in the Nineties, but to prove our point, below here's Kenny from 1975.

Five in 2000 looking like every other boyband.

Boyzone in 1999.

East 17 in 1995.

Blue in 2003.

McFly in 2005.

911 in 1995.

It's not just Brit Boys, this is the American Backstreet Boys in 2000.

Take That in 2007 demonstrating how much of a man band they'd become.

A Lot Less than a Thousand Words

We need a HIT

You'd be forgiven for thinking that this is a band who desperately needed a hit, one just starting out on the rocky road to fame, it is in fact Mud in 1975, who's single Oh Boy had entered the charts the week before and was on it's way to No. 1. Prior to this they'd had six Top 10 hits in a row, two of them reaching the top of the charts. You can imagine the press release – 'ello, 'ello, what have we 'ere then, another smash hit from those cheeky chappies, Mud...

From *the* Archives

The Move

This is The Move in October 1967 on their way to a hearing at the High Court. Their manager, Tony Secunda (third from left), had decided to use a rather tasteless caricature of the then Prime Minister to promote the band's new single, Flowers In The Rain, the possible financial downsides never entered his mind. A month after its release Flowers became the first record to be played on Radio 1 by Tony Blackburn shortly after 7 am on Saturday 30 September 1967. It had reached No. 2, on the charts, only kept from the top by Engelbert's Last Waltz; in theory it had made everyone a good deal of money. Unfortunately Harold Wilson took the offending promotional postcard somewhat to heart and sued Regal Zonophone, the band's label.

The Judge found in favour of the P.M. and he decreed that all royalties from the sale of the record were to be paid to charity, a situation that is still in existence. All rather unfortunate for the song's writer, Roy Wood (second from the right in the photo), who like the rest of the band was unaware of the management's little scheme, as he's never made a penny from the record.

Then & Later On
Cliff Richard

When Cliff had his first hit with Move It in 1958 neither he nor anyone else would have believed it possible that he would still have a career in music fifty years later. Such has been his success that after Elvis Presley he's spent more weeks on the UK singles chart than any other artist. He's unlikely to be caught, his nearest challenger is Elton John and his records have spent the equivalent of ten years less.

Ten things you probably don't know about Cliff

- He was born in Lucknow, India.

- Move It was in part written by Ian Samwell Smith on a bus on the way to Cliff's house.

- According to John Lennon, Move It was the first British rock record.

- He inspired Keith Richards to initially drop the 's' from his surname.

- Devil Woman in 1976 was Cliff's first real US hit.

- It wasn't until 1980 that he changed his name from Harry Webb to Cliff Richard by deed poll.

- Cliff was knighted in 1995 – the first rock star to achieve such a thing.

- In 2002 he was named 52nd in a list of the 100 most important Brits by the BBC.

- According to Cliff because he didn't do 'sex, drugs and alcohol' it makes him the most radical rock and roller.

- In 2006 Cliff received the Portuguese equivalent of a knighthood.

Cliff with Yolande Donlan who starred together in Expresso Bongo in 1959 and again in 2005.

15 July 1985 - Live Aid.

Spot the stars.

February 1975 and Slade have their photograph taken on an antique fire engine. From this point on their chart career went on the slide.

It Seemed Like a Good Idea
at the TIME

In April 1965 The Searchers had their photograph taken with Jane Chidzoy. They'd already had six Top 10 UK hits, including No. 1s. From this point on they failed to crack the UK Top 10 ever again. The question is, who is Jane Chidzoy?

In December 1980 Bob Geldof and 72-year-old grandmother Margaret Laine on a make believe Miami Beach to promote their single, Banana Republic. It was The Boomtown Rat's last Top 10 hit.

In 2004 Adam Ant, who had three No. 1 records, eleven Top 10 hits and twenty-two hit singles in all, is reduced to playing free on a promo gig for 150 people, 'packed' into Our Price Records in Newcastle.

Nat King Cole with Adam Faith in 1960. Ironically Cole died from lung cancer in 1965.

THE UK'S FIRST
Singles Chart

Back in the early Fifties Britain had an aversion to all things decimal which may explain why the chart was actually a Top 12. It was published for the week of 15 November 1952.

1. **Here In My Heart** – Al Martino
2. **You Belong To Me** – Jo Stafford
3. **Somewhere Along The Way** – Nat 'King' Cole
4. **Isle Of Innisfree** – Bing Crosby
5. **Feet Up** – Guy Mitchell
6. **Half As Much** – Rosemary Clooney
7. **High Noon** – Frankie Laine
7. **Forget Me Not** – Vera Lynn
8. **Sugarbush** – Doris Day & Frankie Laine
8. **Blue Tango** – Ray Martin
10. **Auf Wiedersehen (Sweetheart)** – Vera Lynn

11. **Because you're mine** – Mario Lanza
12. **Cowpunchers Cantata** – Max Bygraves
12. **Walking My Way Back Home** – Johnnie Ray

Al Martino at the Savoy Hotel in London, June 1953.

Vera Lynn, 'the Forces sweetheart', during World War 2.

Bing Crosby in 1952; he died after a round of golf in Spain in October 1977.

From *the* **Archives**

Toomorrow

In August 1970 this was a photo call for the band Toomorrow, a group put together by Don Kirschner, the creator of the Monkees, to appear in a film of the same name. It features, Chris Slade (far right), a drummer who was selected from 300 others to join the band – or so it says on the press handout. The other members of the band are Ben Thomas, Vic Cooper and a 21-year-old Olivia Newton-John, making this one of the very first professional pictures of the singer. The film's plot was pretty flimsy and hinged on dying aliens kidnapping the group. Olivia went on to have over twenty British hit singles, including three No. 1s – and who could forget her in Grease?

Olivia was not the only one to find fame; Chris Slade became a very successful drummer who was in AC/DC, Asia and played with Jimmy Page and Dave Gilmour on sessions and albums.

The Neutron bomb with John Travolta while filming Grease.

The 80s
Revisited

Duran Duran

This photograph dates from January 1981 as the band released Planet Earth their first single, which eventually made No. 12 on the charts and the New Romantics were on the way. John Taylor and Nick Rhodes had named their band after the villain in the movie Barbarella. While John and Nick came from Birmingham, as did Roger Taylor the drummer, Simon Le Bon came from London and Andy Taylor from Newcastle – none of the Taylors are related.

Before the year was out they'd cracked the UK Top 10 and went on to become one of the biggest selling bands of the Eighties, with twelve Top 10 records including two No. 1s before the decade was over.

Great Moments in Rock

ROLLING STONES · LET IT BLEED

Back in 1962 Delia was a model; it's her in the front of the five girls.

Not a lot of people know that Delia Smith baked and decorated the cake that appears on the cover of The Rolling Stones Let It Bleed album. 'I was working then as a jobbing home economist, with a food photographer who shot for commercials and magazines. I'd cook anything they needed. One day they said they wanted a cake for a Rolling Stones record cover, it was just another job at the time. They wanted it to be very over-the-top and as gaudy as I could make it!'

The Minister for Culture?

Former Czech President Vaclav Havel was a man known for his penchant for a bit of rock vvvn' roll. He rarely missed the opportunity of catching a gig by visiting bands that included The Rolling Stones. Which is why he may have been persuaded to appoint Frank Zappa as the Czech Republic's Representative for Trade Tourism and Culture in 1991. Unfortunately Frank, who once famously told the audience at a gig at the Royal Albert Hall, 'everyone in this place is wearing a uniform', was a little too free with his advice to his new boss. He said that it was 'unfortunate that President Havel should have to bear the company of someone as stupid as Qualye even for a few minutes.'

Unfortunately Quayle, Dan, was the Vice President of the United States of America; when the US government got wind of it it did little to enhance Frank's reputation in Washington. Instead of D.Q. visiting the President, James Baker, U.S. Secretary of State met with Havel and he was certainly no fan of Mr Z. Apparently at some senate committee that Mr Baker's wife was involved with that was looking into censorship in rock music, she felt that Frank had in some way slighted her. All of this may or may not have counted against the Czech republic's cultural representative, because Mr Z was relieved of his role. No matter how much you like rock, running a country comes first; yet more proof that pop and politics are far from comfortable bedfellows.

POP
and Politics

Pop and politics make uncomfortable bedfellows. There was talk last year that the then Mayor of London, the man formerly known as Red Ken, was thinking of recording with the Cheeky Girls, one of whom was once engaged to Lib Dem MP, Lembit Opik, but more of that later. It's yet another strange tale in the strange business of politicians attempting to 'engage with younger voters' by using pop music, or in some cases simply standing next to pop stars hoping that something may rub off on them.

The Liberals have always fancied themselves as a bit ↑ Liberal Democrats, David Steel, had pop pretensions record called I Feel Liberal – Alright. The song was ac the kilted rocker who lives near David Steel in the Sc with Over the Sea. The cover of the Steel record illus Alright, but somehow you can't imagine anyone, even to get down and par-tee. In 1967 Liberal leader, Jerer pop's pulse and his hands on Jimi's guitar.

Margaret Thatcher emulating The Beatles for some bizarre reason that's gone unrecorded in the history of pop and politics.

Most often the stance of pop has been to attack, through music, the government of the day. It's an activity that goes back to the days of the blues and America's black community and even before that. Few have done it more amusingly than the cast of Spitting Image who in 1984 updated the Phil Spector classic, The Da Doo Ron Ron as a song about Ronald Reagan's bid for re-election in 1984. Two years later Spitting Image had a No. 1 in Britain with The Chicken Song but this was in no way politically motivated. Fortunately for the Tories, Margaret Thatcher was not around when politics went pop because when asked about her favourite song, she unhesitatingly said Telstar by The Tornados.

1983 the then leader of the
his party. He cut an utterly awful
and produced by Jesse Rae
rs. Rae had a minor hit in 1985
ance steps to I Feel Liberal –
disco, getting suitably moved
owed that he had his finger on

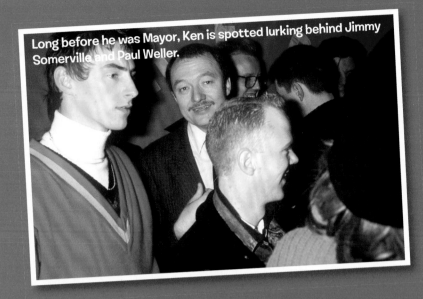

Long before he was Mayor, Ken is spotted lurking behind Jimmy Somerville and Paul Weller.

But it's the Labour Party who really got into the pop groove when they used D-Ream's 1994 No. 1 Things Can Only Get Better as the theme for their 1997 election campaign. There was that rather daft Cool Britannia campaign that saw at least one Gallagher brother in No. 10 Downing Street with the Labour spin meisters attempting to bathe in anyone and everyone's reflected glory. Unfortunately for the Deputy Prime Minister not everyone thought he or Nu-Labour were cool at the 1998 Brit Awards Danbert Nobacon of Chumbawamba threw a bucket of water over John Prescott.

Not the new Labour leader, but Bono speaking at the Party Conference in 2004.

There was one man who mixed pop and politics and was not any good at either of them – the great Screaming Lord Sutch; who was neither a Lord, nor much of a screamer. The founder of the Monster Raving Loony Party stood for parliament over forty times, losing his deposit as often as not.

Whose cheeks are they Anyway?

Lembit Opik, the forty-something Lib Dem politician who represents Montgomeryshire, is of Estonian descent which is possibly what gave him a head start against the competition in gaining the numero uno spot in the affections of Gabriela Irimia, one half (cheek?) of the Cheeky Girls – a popular music group. The political heavyweight and the diminutive pop princess got engaged, to the delight of everyone; sadly this arrangement has since come to an end.

Gabriela and her twin sister Monica come from Transylvania in Romania and against all odds they've managed three British Top 10 singles.

All in all you couldn't make it up.

The Cheeks in 2003, what an earth did he see in her?

More to the point, how did he tell the difference?

Then & Later On
Cat Stevens & Yusuf Islam

Few pop stars have undergone three name changes in their life and none for the kind of deep spiritual reasons that Cat Stevens made his second switch. He started life as Steven Demetre Georgiou, his ancestry is Swedish and Greek Cypriot. His first single, I Love My Dog, gave no indication of the way in which Cat's career would develop, although the follow-up Matthew and Son was a clever and witty song that gave a stronger hint of where his career would progress. Although that and several more of Cat's singles made the Top 10 in the UK it was as an album artist that he became hugely successful, at a time when the album came into it's own and the singer-songwriter was supreme. Throughout much of the Seventies Cat's records were all over the radio, and the charts, but in 1977 he converted to Islam and left music behind to devote his life to educational and philanthropic causes in the Muslim community.

Since then he's been criticised by some, often through misunderstanding the man and his religion, but his music has not been forgotten and is now being rediscovered by a whole new generation of fans. In 2001 he sang his song Peace Train for the first time in twenty years on a video tape that was played at the Concert For New York City; he had earlier condemned the attacks on the Twin Towers. A complex man and a great musician.

Cat in 1970.

Yusuf in 2005.

On 21 August 1967 The Jimi Hendrix Experience arriving at Heathrow Airport from a US tour. Jimi fell foul of the Customs on his return as he was carrying a gas gun. According to Noel Redding, 'It was only a very small gun. It is very mild and is used for personal protection. They're allowed in the States, but according to Customs they're illegal here.'

A Hatchet Job on the Axe Man

In 1983 one of Britain's best-known music journalists, Charles Shaar Murray – a man of strong opinions – went to work on a young, up and coming artist. To give you an idea of his predilections he once called Eric Clapton an 'old fart' whose records made him 'ashamed to be over thirty'. So it probably didn't worry A&M unduly when he was given an album to review by one of their new young artists, a 23-year-old Canadian rock singer and guitarist of whom the company had high hopes. He'd already released a couple of singles that had flirted with the charts in the USA and UK and his new album, Cuts Like a Knife had just entered the American charts.

Murray's review was a total hatchet job. 'This album is a prime example of American rubbish. From the Petty/Springsteen school of Enlightened Rockists. He looks like a cross between Petty and Sting and produces a noise akin to Springsteen writing the worst songs of his career, committing suicide and – as a final act of vengeance – willing the demos to Foreigner. The American charts are bursting wide open to a lot of new music, which raises hopes that rock bores like Adams will find their meal tickets expiring within the near future.' From which we can conclude that Charles was not keen on the new Bryan Adams album. In fairness to Murray the album didn't chart in Britain, although it made No. 8 in America.

However, Adams, without changing his style one jot, has gone on to have over twenty Top 20 singles in Britain (including two No. 1s), four chart-toppers in America, and a whole hat-full of hits. I doubt Charles likes him any more today than he did then.

VERY 70s

This is what it said in the paper in May 1975. 'Sally James, popular hostess of London weekend Television's Saturday morning series Saturday Scene celebrated her 23rd birthday today with top pop stars Alvin Stardust, Peter Shelley and Guys n' Dolls, who gave her a party prior to a live recording of the Saturday Scene Roadshow which was broadcast from the stage of the Wimbledon Theatre. Left to right: Peter Shelley, Alvin Stardust, Sally James and members of the Guys n' Dolls.'

9 January 1977 at the Daily Mirror Pop Awards. From left to right, front row: Joe English, Jimmy McCullough, Denny Laine, Linda and Paul McCartney, David Essex, John Miles. Back row The Rubettes and the Real Thing – 9 January 1977.

From *the* Archives

This is what they told us at the time. . . Julie Ege, the Norwegian film and television actress has started a new career as a pop singer. Her first record – Love, a song by John Lennon – is to be released on the CBS label on 15 January 1971. Julie Ege – one of the worlds most photographed girls – rose to international fame through her part in the Marty Feldman picture, 'Every home should have one'. Since then she has starred in the 'Hammer' film, 'Creatures the world forgot' which is now awaiting release and completed a major role in the film version of 'Up Pompeii'.

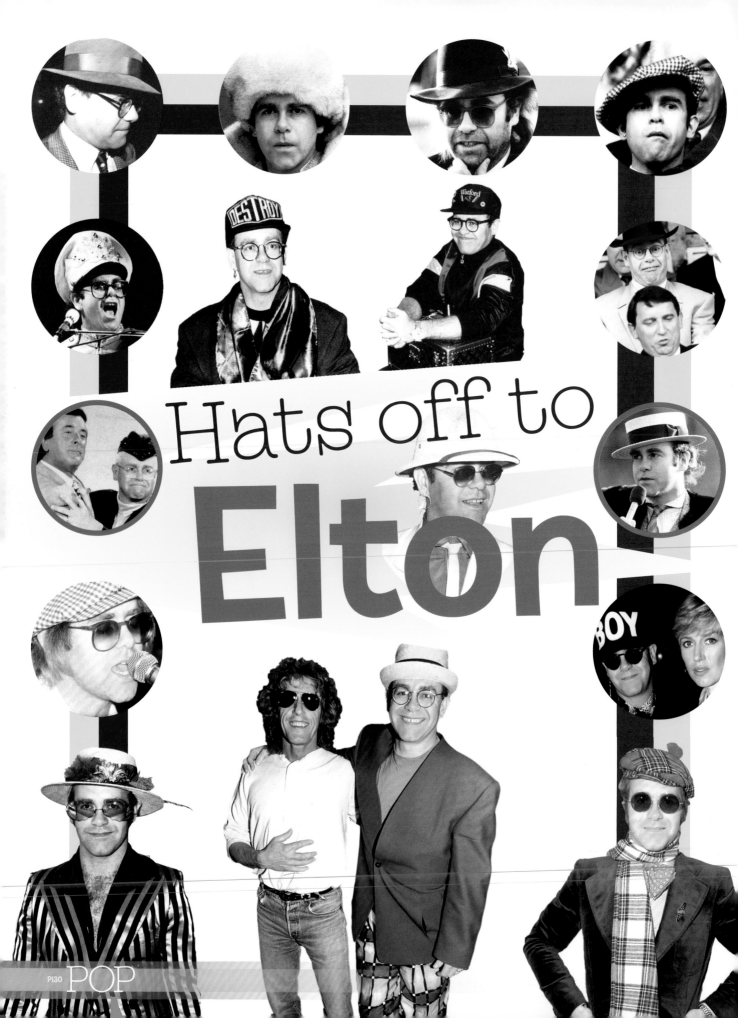

Hats off to Elton

A Red Coat or a Man in Black

Every year old stars are rediscovered and put into that special category reserved for those who have paid their dues. Their back catalogue is trawled for unreleased material and their old albums are remastered; some even get to record new material that as often as not features a duet or two with 'today's top acts'.

Once this is done their careers are reassessed by the leading music critics and the lucky few are put at the top table, as the elder statesmen of not just their genre but of popular music as a whole. Johnny Cash got his seat sometime around 1994 following the release of his highly acclaimed album American Recordings. But just as in life there was darkness before the dawn. In February 1993 Johnny Cash played a weekend booking at Butlin's Holiday Camp in Bognor Regis (half board £61 for the weekend, £26 self catering).

These Butlin's weekends at places like Bognor and Minehead have become a regular off-season filler and as often as not feature 60s shows – some of the bands even have one original member – or Soul weekends, but few have featured legends like the Man in Black. Maybe nobody told him about the last words of King George V...

Not Butlins in Bognor but Falkland Palace in Fife.

Johnny Cash and his wife of a few weeks, June Carter, taken in London in 1968.

Well, which do you think?

Slash (right).

Jimi Hendrix

The Fifty Greatest GUITAR SOLO'S EVER

There's nothing like a list of the greatest anything to kick start a debate, discussion or argument, they can even cause good friends to stop speaking to one another. So here's our contribution...

1. **Stairway to Heaven** - Led Zeppelin - Jimmy Page

2. **Eruption** - Van Halen - Eddie Van Halen

3. **Freebird** - Lynyrd Skynyrd - Gary Rossington & Allen Collins

4. **Comfortably Numb** - Pink Floyd - Dave Gilmour

5. **All Along The Watchtower** - Jimi Hendrix

6. **November Rain** - Guns N Roses - Slash

7. **One** - Metallica - Kirk Hammett

8. **Hotel California** - The Eagles - Joe Walsh & Don Felder

9. **Crazy Train** - Ozzy Osbourne - Randy Rhoads

10. **Crossroads** - Cream - Eric Clapton

11. **Voodoo Chile (Slight Return)** - Jimi Hendrix

12. **Johnny B. Goode** - Chuck Berry

13. **Texas Flood** - Stevie Ray Vaughan

14. **Layla** - Derek & The Dominoes - Eric Clapton & Duane Allman

15. **Heartbreaker** - Led Zeppelin - Jimmy Page

16. **Don't Look Back** - Boston - Tom Scholz

17. **Sharp Dressed Man** - ZZ Top - Billy Gibbons

18. **Europa** - Santana - Carlos Santana

Neil Young.

Dave Gilmour.

Pete Townshend.

Jimmy Page.

Chuck Berry.

Prince.

The Eighties Quiz

1. What was the name of Annie Lennox's group before the Eurythmics?

2. Which American solo singer topped the US charts with seven consecutive singles during the decade?

3. In 1981 an album came out that has spent longer – ten years in all – on the British album charts than any other, what was it?

4. In the Eighties who were the top performing male and female British singers on the American singles chart?

5. In 1989 fifty British music journalists were asked to name their most over-rated artists of the decade. Who was it?

6. Who had more No. 1 singles during the decade, Michael Jackson, Shakin' Stevens, Bros or Duran Duran?

7. In 1985 a British band became the first western group to play a concert in China, who were they?

8. Which well known British super model appeared in a Culture Club video for I'll Tumble 4 Ya before she was famous?

9. Which artist had UK No. 1s with their first three singles in 1983 and '84?

10. In 1982 there was a surprising winner of the Best British Male vocalist at the BRIT awards, who was it?

For the answers see page 208 where you'll also find the names of the performers pictured here.

How not to retire
Gracefully

The world's last count of how many farewell tours Status Quo have done – probably they have too – certainly runs into double figures. But whatever gentle good-natured ribbing we put their way there's no denying that they are, perhaps unbelievably, one of the most successful British bands of all time.

After The Beatles and Queen, they've spent more weeks on the charts than any other group – the equivalent of over eight years. They've had more hit singles than any other British band. They've had twenty-two Top 10 singles in Britain. Thirty-three British hit albums; that's more than any other band, barring The Rolling Stones. So far they've had just one single that reached the top spot – Down Down in 1974. They've had just two American hit singles, but both of those were in 1968!

1977, their tenth anniversary.

The Quo in more recent times.

Then & Later On
Alvin Stardust

The man born Bernard William Jewry in Muswell Hill in 1942 had his first hit in 1961 as Shane Fenton, with his backing band – the Fentones. I'm a Moody Guy made No. 19 in the charts and three more very minor hits followed. He only adopted the pseudonym after the original Shane Fenton died; Bernard had been the band's roadie. By 1965 his career as a pop singer was over and he was making the transition to acting.

In 1973 Bernard returned to pop as Alvin Stardust, a name created by Michael Levy, now Lord Levy, Tony Blair's friend, who at the time owned Magnet Records. My Coo Ca Choo made No. 2 in the UK and a string of hits followed. Today Bernard still pulls on the leathers to perform as Alvin Stardust. The rest of the time he acts and among his many performances he has appeared on the West End stage as the Child Catcher in Chitty Chitty Bang Bang.

Shane Fenton and Iris, a husband and wife who are making a comeback to the stage, seen rehearsing in Sefton Park, Liverpool in 1965.

Gilbert O'Sullivan, Gary Glitter, Alvin Stardust and Rod Stewart on a TV set in January 1975.

Curiosity Killed The Cat pop group singer Ben Volpeliere-Pierrot (left) with Paul Young, Donny Osmond (he thinks it's baseball) and Alvin Stardust playing cricket in 1987.

The 80s Revisted

The Smiths

The Smiths, left to right: Andy Rourke, Mike Joyce (drums), Johnny Marr and Morrissey (front) in March 1984.

The Smiths singer, Morrissey on stage in 1984.

The Smiths were a band that you very definitely had to be of a certain age to 'get'. They first graced the charts in 1983 with This Charming Man, the first in a string of seventeen hit singles, only one of which made the Top 10, a reissue of This Charming Man in 1992. But their success was as an album band and they had seven Top 10 albums, six of which made No. 2 and one, Meat is Murder, topped the UK album charts.

The band was from Manchester and was the total antithesis of the new Romantics – even their name was a deliberate attempt to make themselves seem ordinary. According to the Encyclopaedia Britannica, The Smiths were 'non-rhythm-and-blues, whiter-than-white fusion of 1960s rock and postpunk – a repudiation of contemporary dance.' And there was us thinking they were a pop group...

Fashion DISASTERS

Singer Pete Burns of Dead or Alive.

Andy Bell of Erasure. One word... NO!

Adam Ant promoting his single Apollo 9, which is still no excuse.

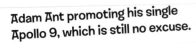

Peter Andre still hoping to get a part in Starlight Express.

Steve Strange, the singer with Visage, in 1981.

Marsha Hunt sings Naked

Record producer Tony Visconti has worked with some of the best in the business – David Bowie, T. Rex, Thin Lizzy, U2, Paul McCartney... and Marsha Hunt. He takes up the story.

One night, very late, Marsha was doing a vocal in Trident Studios mix room. It was one of the last vocals she had to do and it was a song from Hair, the musical in which she appeared. We recorded late at night because she could only record after the show; most nights we started at 11.30 pm Marsha was in the vocal booth off to the side of the mixing console and we could see this lovely woman sing through the booth's window. This particular night she was having a problem, 'feeling the song'. Finally she said, 'I've got it! I usually sing this song naked on stage every night. It feels really weird singing it with clothes on. I'm going to strip.'

Us three blokes in the control room we assumed we were about to die and go to heaven. Marsha was gorgeous; statuesque stacked and had a face that would melt buttah! Marsha soon threw cold water on our collectively rising temperatures.

'You think I want to stand here singing watched by just three randy blokes. I'm happy doing it on stage but this is very different. I want you to tape sheets of newspaper to the window.'

Between takes we heard Marsha light up a cigarette.

'Oh damn, there's no astray in here. Can one of you pass one in?' You've never seen three men move so fast. I got to the door handle first and pulled it, only to feel a lot of resistance. Marsha was a strong lady.

'Hey, no taking a peak. I'll just open the door a crack and you can slide it in sideways.' Funny, that thought crossed my mind too, but I think we were talking about two different things.

Marsha Hunt performing at the Isle of Wight Pop Festival in 1970.

Freddie Mercury in concert at St
James' Park in Newcastle, 1986.

Elvis Presley before a press conference in Germany, March 1962.

Rock ROYALTY

The King – Elvis Presley

King of the Blues – B.B. King, had his first hit in 1951, and is still having them fifty years later

Queen of Soul – Aretha Franklin

Ben E. King – Born a Nelson, joined the Five Crowns who became The Drifters, by which time Benjamin was already a King

Freddie King & Albert King – Blues guitar legends who are no relation to the King of The Blues

Evelyn 'Champagne' King – Former cleaning lady turned Disco Diva

Queen Latifah – American rap star who's real name is Dana Owens

The Kings of Rhythm – Ike Turner's backing band in the Sixties

The Rhythm Kings – Bill Wyman's band after his retirement from The Rolling Stones

The King of Swing – Clarinettist Benny Goodman

Australia's King of Country Music – Slim Dusty

The King of Country Music – Roy Acuff, fiddle player and singer

The Queen of Country Music – Kitty Wells or Reba McEntire, depending on who you believe

The Empress of The Blues – Bessie Smith

King of Ragtime – Scott Joplin

The King of Jazz – A Bing Crosby film with the

Bill Wyman.

Aretha Franklin.

Ike Turner.

King Curtis – Sax player who had hits in his own right and led the Kingpins, the Queen of Soul's backing group

Roy Rogers – The King of the Cowboys

Queen – Topped the British singles chart six times

King Tubby – Former radio repairman Osbourne Ruddock who became a Reggae star

The King Singers – British group singing traditional songs who are probably unknown to every King on the list

Saunders King – One of the first, if not the first, blues electric guitar players

King of Western Swing –Bob Wills

Queen Ida – The first accordion player to lead a Zydeco band

Kingsize Taylor & The Dominoes – Liverpool contemporaries of The Beatles

Pee Wee King – Singer and songwriter, his biggest hit The Tennessee Waltz, his first – Slow Poke

The King of Skiffle – Lonnie Donegan

Wayne King – The unintentionally funny Forties band leader

Terri, Drag Queen of the Blues – Probably self-proclaimed

King of Pop – Michael Jackson, definitely self-proclaimed

Prince – Who'll never be a King no matter what

big production numbers provided by 'The King of Jazz', Paul Whiteman

Brice King – Christian folk singer

The King of Jazz Bass – Charles Mingus

King Oliver's Jazz Band – One of the finest pre-war jazz bands who first recorded in 1923 with Oliver and Louis Armstrong playing the cornet

Nat 'King' Cole – The Sepia Sinatra who had over 100 American hits before he died aged forty-seven in 1965

King – A British dance group from the Eighties

Carole King – The Queen of singer/songwriters

Jonathan King – Who cares

Rev. Martin Luther King – An excerpt from his 'I Had A Dream' speech made No. 88 in the American charts

Queen of Country Blues – Memphis Minnie

Kingdom Come – Arthur Brown's group after he left his Crazy World

Roy Rogers.

Jonathan King.

Benny Goodman.

Nat King Cole.

Then & Later On
Jerry Lee Lewis

Jerry Lee's career never recovered in the UK from the scandal of his child-bride. Whatever his personal life was all about there is no denying that the man known as 'the Killer' was an amazing pianist.

Still going strong forty years on.

Jerry Lee Lewis in May 1958 with his 13-year-old wife Myra in London.

From the **Archives**

The Stranglers

In June 1977 The Stranglers had just had their first minor hit and were on their way towards the UK Top 10 with Peaches/Go Buddy Go. Here we see bass player, Jean Jacques Burnell and guitarist Hugh Cornwall on stage in Manchester. The Stranglers had over thirty UK hit singles and twenty hit albums. They were once described as 'bad-mannered yobs to purveyors of supreme pop delicacies, the group was responsible for music that may have been ugly and might have been crude -- but it was never, ever boring'.

In 1993 Mark Knopfler from Dire Straits was back in his native North East to receive an honorary doctorate from Newcastle University.

Pop Stars taking themselves
VERY SERIOUSLY

Sting after he received an honorary doctorate of Music at the University of Northumbria.

Eurythmics star Dave Stewart having been made an honorary Fellow of Sunderland University in November 1992.

Queen's University Belfast graduation ceremony in July 2001; Van Morrison on his way to receive his honorary doctorate.

Sporty.

Scary.

Posh.

ALL

Spice

In the beginning there was one for every kind of girl...

Baby.

Ginger.

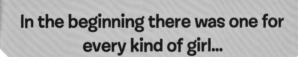

The Spice Women at the o2 Arena for a press conference to announce they are going on a reunion tour.

Daily Mirror — 'ROCK' STAR DIES IN CRASH

The toll: 33 dead 632 injured so far

Daily Mirror — Goodbye, Britain—then the Big Hello

YEAH! YEAH! U.S.A!

IRENE GOES HOME TODAY

5,000 scream 'welcome' to the Beatles

Daily Mirror — Night in jail for Rolling Stone Jagger

BISHOP HALTS 'FILCHED LAND' DEAL

The Six: Gloom in Whitehall

HE AWAITS SENTENCE ON DRUG CHARGE

Daily Mirror — EPSTEIN (The Beatle-Making) Prince of Pop DIES AT 32

"NO WONDER THE MIRROR OUT-SELLS THE FIELD.."

THE QUIET MAN FROM LIVERPOOL WHO RAN A 'STABLE' OF STARS

Mirror — McCartney sues Ringo, John and George

SPLIT UP THE BEATLES SAYS PAUL

Russia reprieves two Jews

AND SO SAY ALL OF US..

HAPPY NEW YEAR

A really HAPPY New Year to all our readers

Mirror — Mayor threatens to call it off

JAGGER WEDDING DAY ROUGH HOUSE

Tug-of-love father: I won't give up baby

Daily Mirror — BRITAIN'S BIGGEST DAILY SALE

Elvis Aron Presley BORN: Tupelo, Mississippi, January 8, 1935 DIED: Memphis, Tennessee, August 16, 1977

In peace at last..

.. the troubled King

SUNDAY Mirror — FORWARD WITH BRITAIN

4am and the cash keeps rolling in

LIVE AID EXTRA

ROCK'S NIGHT OF GLORY

REAGAN — President winning fight for life Full story Page 2

Daily Mirror — FORWARD WITH BRITAIN

Get away from it all WIN! WIN! WIN! A FABULOUS £5000 FORD FIESTA

Great new competition next week

ELTON: IS IT THE END?

Throat op threat to career

...to the Beatles yesterday.

DAILY Mirror — FIRST AGAIN! We're worth £400

FREDDIE THE LAST MOMENTS

By pop legend at his bedside

DOGS KILL BOY OF 9

DAILY Mirror — PEDDLE ME A TICKET!

Michael Jackson yesterday.. picture by Ken Lennox (who else)

DOES THIS LIGHTING SUIT YOU THEN, MR JACKSON?

GUARANTEE This picture is not a fake, not a trick, nor been tampered with in any way. THE ONE YOU BANNED WASN'T EITHER

DAILY Mirror — Get the Jackal — IRA sniper stalks VIPs

THAT'S IT!

3 FREE GOES AT £25m EASTER ROLLOVER PLUS £100,000

Fans in tears as Take That say goodbye

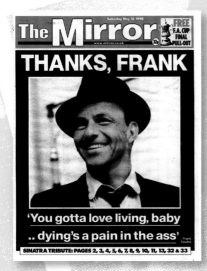

The Mirror — FREE F.A. CUP FINAL PULL-OUT

THANKS, FRANK

'You gotta love living, baby .. dying's a pain in the ass'
— Frank Sinatra

SINATRA TRIBUTE: PAGES 2, 3, 4, 5, 6, 7, 8, 9, 10, 11, 13, 32 & 33

The Mirror — EXCLUSIVE: My love for Debbie by England hero David Seaman

Fayed: Why I blasted Diana's mother

STONES AXE TOUR IN PROTEST AT BLAIR

Band's anger over £10m tax bill

WILMA FOUND!

The Mirror — Help design Diana memorial

MIRROR READERS INVITED TO SEND IN THEIR IDEAS: PAGE 7

Racist scare Hague is new Enoch

MADONNA SACKS HER BUTLER

He will sue for £100,000

Liz earns herself a ticket

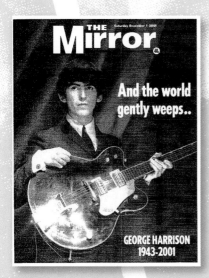

THE Mirror

And the world gently weeps..

GEORGE HARRISON 1943-2001

DAILY Mirror — DAME ELLEN'S DIARY

Man Utd thugs in threat to Glazer

MY LAST CHANCE

Blair told to call a snap election

Kate Moss' junkie lover is freed..and pledges: 'If I don't kick drugs I'll die'

DAILY Mirror — A BETTER READ, GUARANTEED

THE DIANA DOSSIER
SENSATIONAL NEW EVIDENCE: PAGES 8&9

GEORGE MICHAEL 'CANNABIS' ARREST

CARELESS SPLIFFER

Star found slumped over wheel of his car

Is LIZ having a BABY?

£60m HEIST HELL

...the Press con

Ten each from John & Paul

John on stage in Derbyshire in 1963.

Ten 'Lennon & McCartney' compositions solely written by:

Paul	John
Love Me Do,	Please, Please Me,
All My Loving,	I Feel Fine,
Yesterday,	Day Tripper,
Paperback Writer,	In My life,
Here, There, Everywhere,	Lucy In The Sky With Diamonds,
With A Little Help From My Friends,	I Am The Walrus,
Hello Goodbye,	A Hard Day's Night,
Get Back,	If I fell,
Lady Madonna,	Ticket To Ride,
Penny Lane	Help

Paul sings Yesterday at Blackpool in August 1965.

THE BEATLES

THE BEAT Svengali

Larry 'the Beat Svengali' Parnes was an old fashioned manager of pop stars; he was dubbed 'Mr Parnes, Shillings and Pence' which gives you some idea of where Larry was coming from. Mr Parnes' theory of guaranteed stardom was simple; you needed the right sounding name. Unlike Americans, whose real names always sounded right, post-war Britain suffered from a plethora of Rons, Toms, Johns and even a few Clives. In fact Larry's inspiration was Rock Hudson, which probably tells you something about Mr Parnes. Once a young hopeful was signed to Larry's 'stable of stars' he was quickly given a name that would look equally at home on a marquee or a Parlophone or Pye 45 rpm single.

John Askew – Johnny Gentle

Dave Nelson – Vince Eager

Ray Howard – Duffy Power

Richard Knellor – Dickie Pride

Thomas Hicks – Tommy Steele

Ronald Wycherley – Billy Fury

Reginald Smith – Marty Wilde

Clive Powell – Georgie Fame

There were a very few that got away with a name change, including Peter Wynne. One young man was told he was going to be called Elmer Twitch, somehow common sense prevailed and he stayed plain old Joe Brown.

Joe Brown (left) with Gene Pitney.

Dickie Pride.

Georgie Fame.

Kim Wilde's Mum and Dad.

The Rolling Stones Rock 'n' Roll Circus, December 1968.

Robbie Williams in concert at Wembley Arena in 1998.

Robbie hugs Clara Bruni, the future French first lady, at the MTV Awards at Zenith, Paris in November 1995.

100% ROBBIE

Great talent, clown, showman, stellar entertainer, troubled artist, Robbie is loved by millions and many are waiting for the next phase in a career that could never be described as boring.

Robbie Williams with Take That in concert Glasgow 1994.

Robbie Williams dressed as Elvis for a video shoot in Blackpool.

Robbie Williams filming a 7-Up advert.

Robbie Williams at the window of his apartment in 2002.

Robbie Williams at the SECC Glasgow February 1999.

Robbie in July 1997.

The 80s
Revisited

Shakin' Stevens

It's easy to write off the man who first charted in the UK just as the Eighties were beginning; Shakey's seen posing in Birmingham in June 1980 having had one minor hit. No one could have predicted what a huge star he would become. He had thirty hits in all during the decade – much against the musical grain – including three No. 1s and eleven other Top 10 hits. But Mr S. was no overnight success. Back in 1970 he recorded, Spirit of Woodstock which sunk without trace; it wasn't helped when it was reviewed as it got a big thumbs down. Shakey was incensed, we know this because he wrote the following week to the music paper's letters page, the inspiringly named 'Pop Post', to complain. He said, 'He got it all wrong. . . What did David Hughes [the reviewer] want? Sumertime Blues, one more time?' Shakey finished off with 'flower power is dead, while rock keeps rolling along'. The letter was signed Shakin' Stevens, Queen's Road, Penarth, Glamorgan.

Before *they were* Famous

REM

When this photograph was taken back in 1986, REM – which of course stands for Rapid Eye Movement – were relatively unknown in Britain, although the band from Athens, Georgia had managed to crack the US charts with three singles, the most successful, Radio Free Europe reaching the dizzy heights of No. 75. It came out in Britain and a reviewer in one music paper said, 'In a week largely unsullied by decent records this is... reasonable.' It failed to chart and it would be another four years until The One I Love just failed to make the Top 50 in 1987.

Then & Later On
The Monkees

Hey, hey we're The Monkees... They hit the charts by way of our TV screens in January 1967 and you'll probably be surprised that they only had one British No. 1 single – their debut, I'm A Believer, which was written by Neil Diamond. It all dried up for them two years later, but they've managed a number of comeback tours to capitalise on their one million minutes of fame.

Left to right: Mike Nesmith, Mickey Dolenz and Davy Jones in 1997.

From left to right: Davy Jones, Peter Tork, Mike Nesmith and Mickey Dolenz in London 1967.

Fantasy
TOP OF THE POPS

The Byrds, left to right: Roger McGuinn, Kevin Kelley, Gram Parsons and Chris Hillman in May 1968.

Have you ever thought that some record labels would read better, but maybe not sound better, if someone else had recorded them? Here are some No. 1 records that definitely fit the bill.

Steps.

Two Little Boys – Ant & Dec
99 Red Balloons – Puff Daddy
A Whiter Shade Of Pale – Cream
I'm A Believer – Cliff Richard
Diamonds – Jewel
Return To Sender – The Singing Postman
Nut Rocker – Ozzy Osbourne
The Young Ones – The Rolling Stones
Flying Without Wings – Pilot
Frozen – Freez
Barbie Girl – Barbra Streisand
Walking On The Moon – Steps
Knockin' On Heaven's Door – Judas Priest
A Picture Of You – Altered Images

Mr Vain – Carly Simon
Tears On My Pillow – Tears For Fears
Hold Me Close – Squeeze
He Ain't Heavy, He's My Brother – Karen Carpenter
Doctor in The Tardis – The Who
I'm Your Man – Boy George
West End Girls – East 17
Billie Jean – King
Happy Talk – Talk Talk
Ebony & Ivory – Russ Conway
No Charge – Free
Little Red Rooster – Chicken Shack
Can The Can – Can
Chirpy Chirpy Cheep Cheep – The Byrds

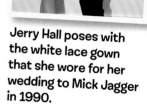

Jerry Hall poses with the white lace gown that she wore for her wedding to Mick Jagger in 1990.

Karen and Richard Carpenter in 1973.

Billie Piper marries Chris Evans in Las Vegas in 2001.

Billie Piper has another go, this time with Laurence Fox in 2007.

More POP Weddings

Elton John with his wife Renate Blauel on their wedding day.

Ronnie Wood marries Jo Howard in 1985 with best men Charlie Watts and Keith Richard.

Kirsty MacColl at her Wedding to Steve Lillywhite in August 1984 with her father the folk singer, Euan.

Peter Hook, who was in Joy Division, marries Becky Jones 1997.

Kate Moss (right) and Chrissie Hynde of the Pretenders in August 2003 on their way to Stella McCartney's wedding.

David Beckham and wife Victoria Beckham sitting on thrones used at their wedding in July 1999.

Dave Dee & Simon Dee

Dave Dee, Nicki Hamilton, Suzy Bryant and Simon Dee at the Pop Ahead to 1977 party at the Royal Lancaster Gate Hotel in November 1967.

Dave and Simon were of course no relation and it's unclear who took up with the surname first, although it was probably Simon. Dave was the lead singer of Dave Dee, Dozy, Beaky Mitch and Titch who had their first hit at the end of 1965. Dave's first brush with pop was as a policeman in Wiltshire when he was one of the first people on the scene of the car crash in which Eddie Cochran died. Besides continuing to tour Dave Dee has become a Justice of the Peace so neatly bringing his life full circle in the eyes of the law.

Cyril Nicholas Henty-Dodd, as Simon was christened, had been the first voice to be heard in Radio Caroline in 1964. His success encouraged BBC radio to offer him a job and he hosted his own show on the Light programme. By the time this photograph was taken Simon was hosting his own evening TV show, Dee Time, and was enjoying huge success. His decline was a lot faster than his rise and he disappeared from our TV screens after a bizarre interview with the actor George Lazenby who it's said had smoked a joint prior to appearing. After some abortive attempts to kick start his career on local radio Simon disappeared altogether before Victor Lewis Smith did a one off Dee Time for Channel 4 in 2003.

They did it FIRST

At least Ozzy had the good sense (?) to dangle his son Jack from his teeth while not leaning over a hotel balcony.

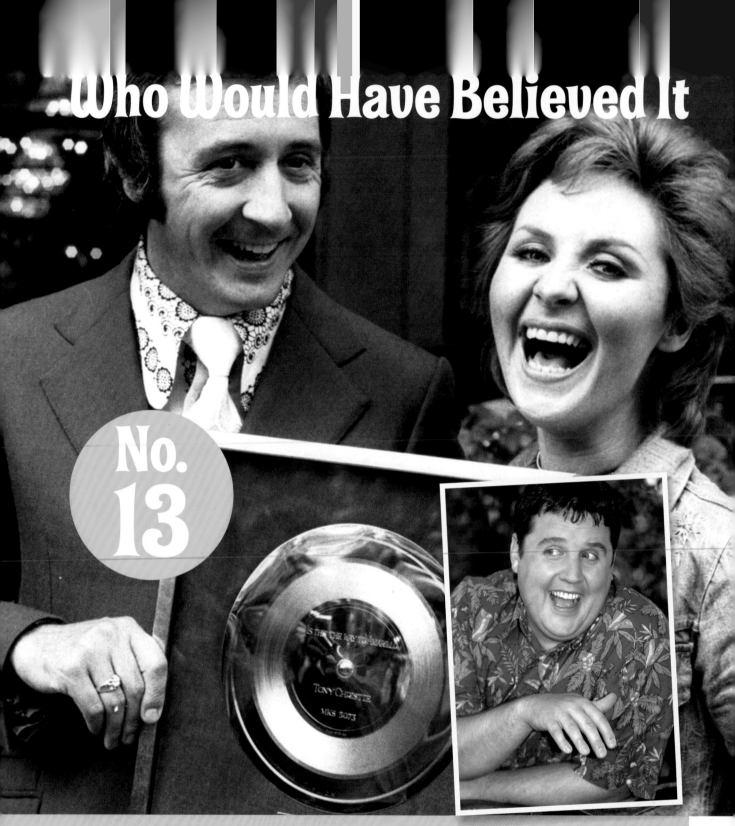

Who Would Have Believed It

No. 13

If you'd have told Tony Christie that he would be at No. 1 thirty-something years later with Is This The Way to Amarillo he'd probably have thought you daft. The first time around it actually only made No. 18, but he still got a gold disc for a million sales, pictured here with the ubiquitous Lulu in 1972. Of course it was all down to the comedian Peter Kay. . .a pop anorak and one of the funniest men in Britain, that it happened for Tony all over again.

The artist formerly known as Prince, when he was still known as Prince, although now he's back to being Prince once again.

David Gray in concert in 2002.

In 1992 a young singer/songwriter issued a single called Birds Without Wings on the Hut Label. By the end of 1994 he had issued a couple more and released two albums. None of them failed to trouble the charts. In December 1994 Johnny Black writing in Mojo said, 'he delivers in spades.' He, like many others in the know was tipping the singer for bigger things. Even Joan Baez who had seen him on TV said of his writing 'the best lyrics since a young Bob Dylan.' It took another six years before David Gray found acceptance with the public at large. His 1998 album White Ladder finally topped the UK album charts in August 2001.

The 80s
Revisited

Eurythmics

Annie Lennox
in 1983.

In February 1983 Nick Rhodes was invited to be a guest reviewer in one of the pop papers, Hungry Like A Wolf, Save A Prayer and Rio had all graced the Top 10 in the previous year and Duran Duran were hot. Among the singles was a new one from a band who had had two records that just managed to scrape into the Top 75 in the previous two years. Their new song Sweet Dreams (Are Made Of This) was, according to the Duranie keyboard player of, 'Little substance. . .it passes without noticing. I've already forgotten how it goes and don't expect to be remembering it in the near future. It lacks excitement and feeling waiting for the mega hook to no avail.' It was of course the record that broke the Eurythmics, making No. 2 in the UK and topping the US charts.

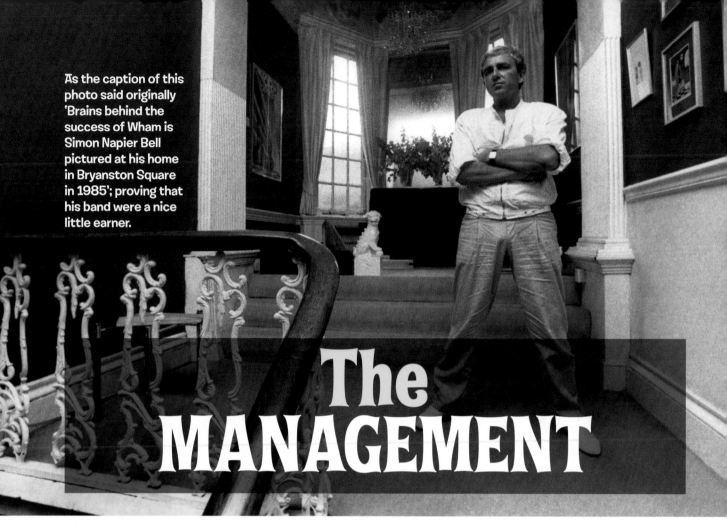

As the caption of this photo said originally 'Brains behind the success of Wham is Simon Napier Bell pictured at his home in Bryanston Square in 1985'; proving that his band were a nice little earner.

The MANAGEMENT

It's the management what did it! How big a part do the managers play in their young charge's success. Well ask any of this lot and they'd probably say an awful lot... and to be fair all of them would probably have a good point.

Malcolm McLaren, Svengali of the Sex Pistols.

The man who nearly was king. Giorgio Gomelsky was the first, though unofficial, manager of the Stones. He lost out to Andrew Loog Oldham and then went onto manage The Yardbirds with Eric Clapton.

Don Arden with his son David in their office in 1989.

Don was not a man to be trifled with. His reputation for being the toughest manager in the music business was well earned and well maintained. He was also the father of Sharon who later became Mrs Ozzy Osbourne – Don gave her Ozzy's management contract as a wedding present.

Then & Later On
Boy George

Without doubt one of the voices of Eighties pop, Boy George of Culture Club. Here he's pictured with Alison Moyet at the Rock and Pop Awards in 1983. With five top three singles already behind him he was unstoppable. Culture Club enjoyed huge success in America.

In 2007 George O'Dowd was charged with falsely imprisoning a man and appeared in court. Life had become very different for the man who once famously said, 'I prefer a nice cup of tea to sex with boys and/or girls'.

The Escorts play the Cavern Club in Liverpool where The Beatles had made their name.

Stars
and their Homes

Match the stars to their homes!
Couldn't be simpler.

For answers see page 208.

5

6

7

From *the* **Archives**

The Yardbirds

According to the newspaper reports at the time 'a group of Mods descended on Lord Willis' home after he'd made remarks in the House of Lords about modern music.' In fact the whole thing was a setup created by the band's PR man. It was 1964, The Yardbirds had just formed and this was to help further their career. The very young, rather smart, short haired, chap on the left of the picture playing guitar is Eric Clapton. Paul Samwell-Smith is next to Eric, the singer is Keith Relf, on drums is Jim McCarty and on the right of the picture is Chris Dreja.

VERY 70s

In 1975 a war of words broke out in the press between two bands claiming to be the original Guys 'n' Dolls. In fact there were three bands that could lay claim to the name. Their early recordings were in fact recorded by session singers, two of whom are pictured below; Clare Torry was the voice on Pink Floyd's Great Gig in the Sky from The Dark Side of the Moon album.

The so-called original Guys and Dolls; they had an and not a 'n'.

Left to right: David Van Day, Tereza Bazar, Dominic Grant, Martine Howard, Paul Griggs and Julie Forsyth who appeared on our TV screens as Guys 'n' Dolls singing There's A Whole Lot of Loving in March 1975. In 1977 David Van Day and Tereza Bazar left the band and became Dollar.

Two session singers, Kay Garner and Clare Torry in the studio in March 1975.

Then & Later On
The Jam

The Jam were one of the most successful groups of the 1980s, having four UK No. 1 singles and a whole string of other hits, including six Top 10 albums. The Jam disbanded in 1982 and Paul Weller went on to form The Style Council who never managed a No. 1 single but did have seventeen hit records on the singles chart. As a solo artist Paul's success has mainly been with albums, which include 1995's Stanley Road that went to No. 1 and spent 87 weeks in the charts.

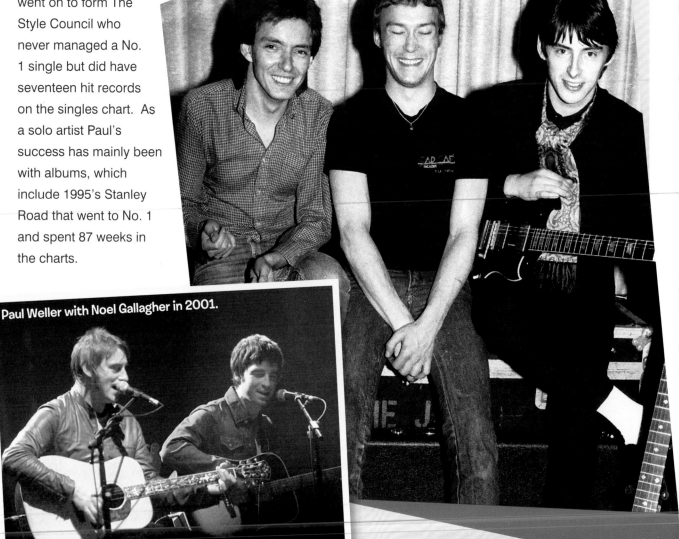

Paul Weller with Noel Gallagher in 2001.

The Jam in 1980 as Going Underground is on its way to No. 1 – Bruce Foxton, Rick Buckler and Paul Weller.

Fashion DISASTERS

A Beatles dress sold by C&A in 1964. I wonder what it would fetch on eBay?

Gilbert O'Sullivan. February 1975; looking very Starsky or is it Hutch?

Ginger Baker of Cream looking the part.

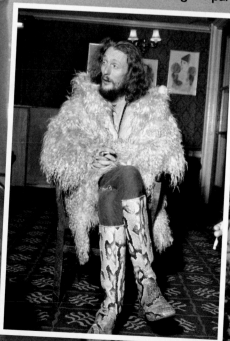

Then & Later On
David Bowie

Before he found fame as David Bowie, David Jones as he was known plugged away releasing a whole string of singles, many of which fetch huge prices from collectors of rare vinyl. By 1969 he'd become David Bowie, started working with producer Tony Visconti and begun to reinvent his image – the first of many such image changes. The below photo was taken in June 1971 shortly before superstardom set in and it shows Bowie's wife Angie and their three-week-old son Zowie.

The Nineties And Beyond Quiz

1. Which British band went to No. 2 in America and then spent a whole year on the singles chart with Missing?

2. Two singles spent longer at No. 1 on the charts than any other record since Frankie Laine's 1950's hit, I Believe. Neither artist was English. Name the artists and their singles.

3. In 1999 a British singer became the second oldest to ever top the UK charts, who was it?

4. Geri Halliwell, Gary Barlow, Ronan Keating and Mel C. Who's had the most No. 1 singles as a solo artist?

5. Which British diva from the Sixties starred at Glastonbury in 2007?

6. Which band is second to Elvis Presley with the most double –A side hit singles in Britain?

7. Which American solo singer, who started having hits in 1986 and carried on throughout the Nineties and beyond, has had almost forty hits but never a British No. 1?

8. Which British band has spent more weeks at No. 1 on the UK singles chart other than The Beatles?

9. Who's written the most No. 1 singles, Gary Barlow, Michael Jackson or Mick Jagger?

10. Which band was at No. 1 when the new millennium came to pass?

Geri Halliwell.

Gary Barlow.

Ronan Keating.

For the answers see page 208.

Soap Stars/ Pop Stars

You'd be forgiven for thinking that soap stars making records and having hits was something that first occurred in the 1980s, but you couldn't be more wrong. Back in 1961 John Leyton appeared on the popular ITV drama, Harpers West One as Johnny St Cyr singing Johnny Remember Me to an estimated viewing audience of 25 million people. It was voted best single of the year in the annual New Musical Express poll. Since then just about every soap seems to have spawned a pop star.

John Leyton with Mia Farrow in 1964.

Jennie Moss played Lucile in Coronation Street, with her is Bob Lang of the Mindbenders. Her debut single, Hobbies, produced by Joe Meek, was released in June 1963, but despite a weekly audience of 34 million, the single failed to chart, although she didn't perform it on the series.

Home and Away actor Daniel Amalm at a CD signing in Gateshead.

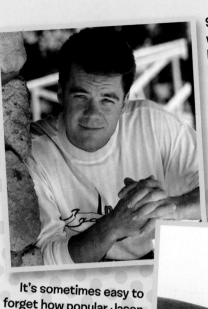

Stefan Dennis who plays Paul Robinson in Neighbours had two minor hits in 1989.

It's sometimes easy to forget how popular Jason Donovan was. He had four British No. 1 singles and another six Top 10 records. His first album went to No. 1 and spent a year on the charts.

Everyone knows of Dame Kylie's success but don't forget Craig McLachlan who also appeared in Neighbours. He went to No. 2 in the UK with Mona in 1990 and had limited success with another half dozen singles.

Martine McCutcheon in 2000, shortly after her UK No. 1 Perfect Moment. She'd starred in Eastenders but was killed off in 1998.

Take me to the PILOT

Performing with Iron Maiden in 1985.

When Bruce Dickinson joined Iron Maiden in late 1981, he played his first gig in Italy after driving 36 hours in a van to get there. He must have scarcely imagined that twenty years later he would be flying to the Mediterranean, and not just as a passenger but also as the pilot of a Boeing 737 belonging to British charter airline Astreus. After enjoying twelve years with Iron Maiden Bruce left in 1993, citing the inevitable musical differences. Bruce pursued a solo career and took up flying seriously, gaining his commercial pilot's license. He did get back with Maiden in 1999 but not before he began flying for an airline. On one occasion, after a flight, he was in uniform in Munich airport and he was accosted by a German Iron Maiden fan in full battle dress (Tour T-shirt, cross, etc). 'Hello? But I must know. . .is this the bus to Munich?' The Maiden reunion spawned a number of hits including Wicker Man, which meant that Bruce was the first airline pilot to have a Top 10 record on the UK singles chart.

Then & Later On
David Essex

David Essex's first single was the brilliant Rock On and he'd come to fame after starring in the musical Godspell in 1971, before appearing in the movie That'll Be The Day. His good looks created a huge following among female fans and this, combined with really well crafted pop records, gave him a very busy career throughout the Seventies. Despite things slowing in the Eighties he still pulled off some solid success with singles that included A Winter's Tale and Silver Dream Machine.

1974.

2007.

TEN SONGS
About Famous People

Football's first pop star – George Best in 1970.

Rosanna – Toto (Rosanna Arquette)

You're in my Heart – Rod Stewart (Britt Ekland)

Uptown Girl – Billy Joel (Christie Brinkley)

Belfast Boy – Don Fardon (George Best)

Candle in the Wind – Elton John (Marilyn Monroe)

Less Than Zero – Elvis Costello (Oswald Mosley)

Linda – Jan & Dean (Linda Eastman before she became Linda McCartney)

Shine on you Crazy Diamond – Pink Floyd (Syd Barrett)

Pride (In the Name of Love) – U2 (Martin Luther King)

And of course You're so Vain by Carly Simon... the consensus is Warren Beatty, but of course Mick Jagger, probably thinks it's about him; he also sings on it.

Britt Ekland with Peter Sellers, her first husband.

Martin Luther King gets an honorary doctorate at Newcastle University in 1967.

Rosanna Arquette.

Marilyn Monroe with her husband, the playwright, Arthur Miller.

Warren Beatty.

We think of charity gigs and pop stars as an Eighties phenomenon but back in the winter of 1963 the stars came out for Oxfam. They did a tour of the West End on a float and ended up singing Christmas carols under the Christmas tree in Trafalgar Square. Left to right: Bert Weedon, Dickie Valentine, Penny Forsyth, Bruce Forsyth, Craig Douglas, Alan Freeman, Pearl Carr, Teddy Johnson (Hidden), Dennis King of the King Brothers.

More
Pop stars and their
Cars!

Mike Nesmith of The Monkees with his wife as their newly purchased Mini Cooper S is delivered to their hotel in July 1967.v

Tom Jones shows off his new Jaguar in April 1966.

ECD 131 C

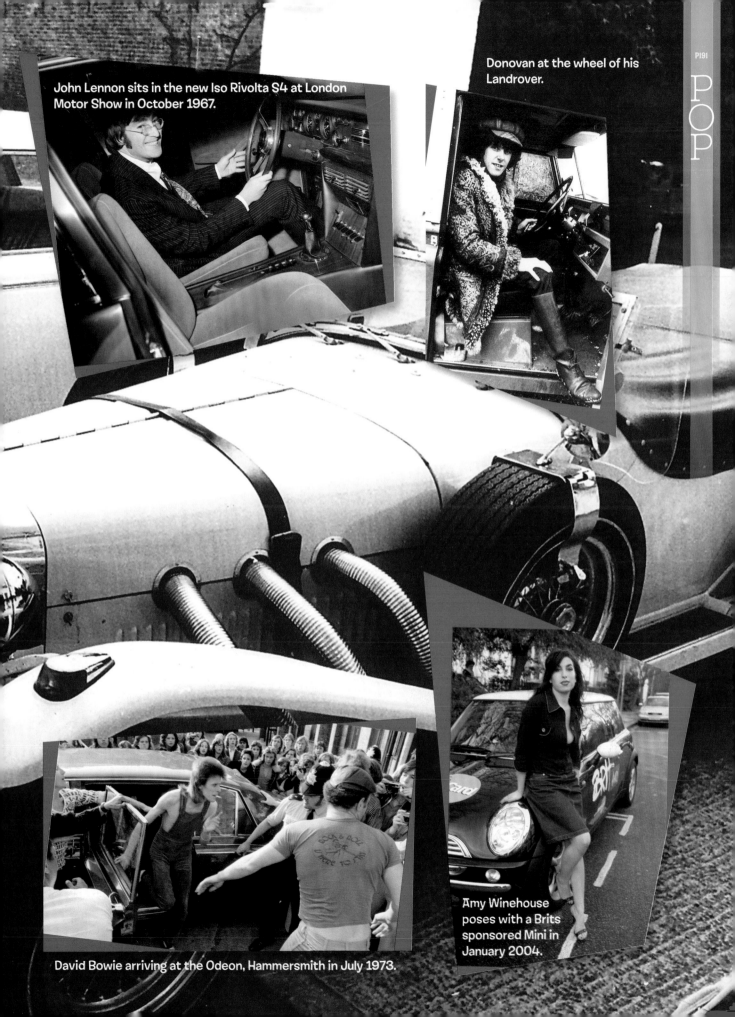

John Lennon sits in the new Iso Rivolta S4 at London Motor Show in October 1967.

Donovan at the wheel of his Landrover.

David Bowie arriving at the Odeon, Hammersmith in July 1973.

Amy Winehouse poses with a Brits sponsored Mini in January 2004.

Phil Everly on stage in October 1962. Don and Phil, The Everly Brothers, always crafted great sounding pop songs that sound as good today as they did fifty years ago. Their timeless recordings took them to the top of the UK charts four times and made them models for many aspiring musicians in the beat boom. This rare shot of just Phil Everly on stage at the Granada Cinema in East Ham, London was because his brother was recovering from food poisoning in a London hospital.

From the Archives

The Osmonds

The Osmond Brothers pose with their bodyguards dressed as city gents in August 1974. This was at the time when they had their only UK No. 1 single – Love Me For A Reason. They are another of those bands that somehow you think of as having many more chart-topping records; they did manage four more Top 10 hit singles. Of course Donny did have three solo No. 1s and Little Jimmy had one too. As a family, including sister Marie they had over thirty hits between them.

Leicester City's Frank Worthington sings with The Grumbleweeds at Bailey's Club in Leicester in 1975.

Paul Gascoigne with Lindisfarne promoting their single Fog On The Tyne in 1990.

Football POP

For some strange reason football and pop have always been strange bedfellows. Today with footballers being more like pop stars, the gulf seems to have widened – which all goes to prove it's a funny ol' game.

Brighton and Hove Albion captain Steve Foster, Buster Bloodvessel of Bad Manners, and Michael Robinson in 1982.

Don Fardon at George Best's boutique in Manchester to help promote his new record Georgie, in March 1970.

Tottenham Hotspur's Clive Allen recording the Spurs song before the 1987 FA Cup Final with Chas and Dave.

Elton John with Maurice 'Mo' Johnston who played for Watford before signing for Celtic.

I bet you had no idea that Brian Clough was a Sinatra fan. This was in 1964 when he was still playing for Sunderland. It's often overlooked what a great goal scorer he was before his career was cut short through injury. He scored 54 times for Sunderland in 61 appearances and 197 times for Middlesbrough in 213 appearances.

Robbie Williams with his former Take That band mate, Mark Owen, in 1997.

Yet More Stars and their Homes

Simply tell us who lives where...

For answers see page 208.

Delaney (third right) and Bonnie (second right) and friends with their two best friends being Eric Clapton (seated) and George Harrison (third from left) and the rest of their band at the Colston Hall in Bristol in December 1969.

Then & Later On
Fleetwood Mac

Fleetwood Mac arriving at Heathrow Airport from the USA in February 1970 after a three-month tour. Peter Green, the band's major songwriter and a brilliant guitarist, is second from the left. This was shortly before Green left the band; he had his drink spiked with LSD which badly affected his somewhat fragile mental state. Left is Jeremy Spencer, behind Green is Mick Fleetwood, next is Danny Kirwan and right is John McVie. After many changes in personnel the band became the archetypal Seventies rock band with Fleetwood and McVie remaining from the original line-up with Americans Lindsey Buckingham and Stevie Nicks joining in 1975; Christine Perfect who married McVie joined in 1970.

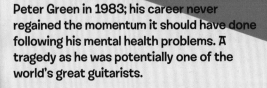

Peter Green in 1983; his career never regained the momentum it should have done following his mental health problems. A tragedy as he was potentially one of the world's great guitarists.

Jimmy Saville with The Shadows in 1964.

Telly Savalas with Michael Aspel in April 1975 – Kojak had had a No. 1 with If.

The Platter SPINNERS

Those brave and intrepid fellows who used to spin the platters that matter, shape the musical taste of the nation and now simply press buttons on computers and tell us about the weather...

Never one to shy away from controversy, the late, great, Kenny Everett on the picket line with musicians on strike to save BBC live music in June 1980.

Tony Blackburn, dressed as a woman, with fellow Radio 1 DJ's David 'Kid' Jenson, Andy Peebles, Paul Burnett, Peter Powell and Simon Bates.

Kate Bush with David 'Kid' Jensen in 1979.

John Peel in 1968.

Bros with Mark Goodier in 1985.

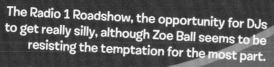

The Radio 1 Roadshow, the opportunity for DJs to get really silly, although Zoe Ball seems to be resisting the temptation for the most part.

The 80s
Revisited

Having been around on our charts since 1982 you'd have thought by 1986 that Wham! would have decided the need to dress in somewhat bizarre fashions was over – but no! A few months later they had their final concert at Wembley stadium in June before George went off to be a mega star and Andrew just went off. By the end of 1987 George's first solo album was ready to unleash on the world. George had also topped the charts earlier in 1987 in both the UK and the USA with I Knew You Were Waiting, a duet with Aretha Franklin, so everyone had great faith in George.

A reviewer for one of the pop magazines quickly set his fingers tapping on the keyboard to give us his views. 'George Michael himself used to identify why Wham! were so successful. They had good songs of course, but beyond that they knew how to be pop stars. Faith is, I fear, a reaction to Wham! and sadly in making it he seems to have thrown the baby (his song writing talent) out with the bathwater (Wham!). Whatever the reason it's an uneven largely dull affair.' He then goes on to rubbish every track on the album, even comparing George Michael to 'Shakin' Stevens on a good day' before closing with the immortal words, 'maybe he should have stuck with Andrew Ridgeley after all.' He rated the album as two stars, which Q deemed to be 'poor'. Faith of course was an enormous selling album. It went to No. 1 in Britain and spent 77 weeks on the charts, spawning six UK hit singles. All this though pales compared to George's success in America. Faith topped the album chart, sold over ten million copies, won a Grammy as album of the year, provided George with six hit singles, all of which went Top 10; four of these topped the US Hot 100. The album made George Michael a worldwide star.

Andrew Ridgeley divides his time between Monaco and Hertfordshire.

Then & Later On
Petula Clark

As a child star Petula began her career entertaining the troops in the Second World War and had her first hit on the UK charts with The Little Shoemaker in 1954. A number of other hits followed in the Fifties and she had her first No. 1 with Sailor in 1961. It was in 1964 when she teamed up with writer Tony Hatch that her career really took off. She had a huge worldwide hit in 1964 with Downtown and followed it with many other great pop songs that have stood the test of time. Later she moved into musical theatre and still tours today to enthusiastic audiences.

Petula in 1958 with Joe Henderson.

Petula in 2001.

From *the* **Archives**

Michael Fagan

Michael Fagan, no relation to Donald Fagen who is one half of Steely Dan and spells his name differently, was the man who broke into Buckingham Palace in 1982 only to sit on the Queen's bed for a ten-minute chat. Eventually, after much royal bell ringing, a policeman arrived – he'd been walking the corgis – and Mr Fagan was arrested; however, no charges were brought. A year later he, along with the punk band The Bollock Brothers, covered The Sex Pistols, God Save The Queen – it lived up to their name...

Tales from the Indian Ocean

Before the lure of King Arthur on ice Rick Wakeman was known to enjoy much simpler pleasures while a member of the Seventies rock band Yes; of whom he once said, 'they were going towards the cosmic stratosphere and I was going down the Dog and Duck.' When he left the band in 1974 he did so under a bit of a cloud, or to be perfectly correct a bit of a smell. One night at Manchester's Free Trade Hall, during the interminably long Tales From Topographic Oceans, Rick felt a little peckish and suggested to his roadie that a curry wouldn't go a miss. And not just a curry, but chicken vindaloo, Bombay aloo, bindi bhaji, stuffed paratha, pilau rice and six poppadoms. Rick's roadie duly beat a path to a local curry house and no sooner was he away but back, by which time they were only up to side three of Topographic Oceans. At this point Rick's keyboards were not featuring and so he set about his Indian (having not expected it to arrive until after the show). Very quickly the rest of the band noticed the smell, and so apparently did the audience. At which point diminutive lead singer, Jon Anderson, leans over the keyboard, 'Bloody hell Rick, you've got a curry.' Rick's reply was equally to the point, 'I'm bored.' When the tour ended Rick left Yes, but he would be back... several times.

The seven ages of Madonna

Since Madonna first appeared on the UK charts in early 1984 urging us to Holiday, it's been anything but for her hairdresser. How many other pop stars have changed their hairstyle and colour so often. . . OK, other than David Bowie?

The Bikini Years – 1993.

The Film Star with George Harrison 1986.

The Mrs Peron Years – 1995.

Back To The Black Years – 1998.

The Basque Years 1985.

The Mexican Madge Years – 2000.

The Victorian Years – 2006.

Answers to Fifties Quiz

Frankie Laine (19)

Move It

Acker Bilk

I Believe – Frankie Laine, Rose Marie – Slim Whitman & Cara Mia – David Whitfield

The Stargazers, Bill Haley & His Comets, The Dreamweavers, The Crickets and Lord Rockingham's XI

I Believe – Frankie Laine

Emile Ford & the Checkmates – What Do You Want To Make Those Eyes At Me For

Jimmy Young

Winifred Atwell & Russ Conway

Winifred Atwell

Pictures: Frankie Laine, David Whitfield, Slim Whitman & Acker Bilk

Answer to Spot the Oldest

– Debbie Harry

Answers to Sixties Quiz

Louis Armstrong aged 67 years and 10 months

Helen Shapiro

Manfred Mann

Eddie Cochran

Simon & Garfunkel – The Sound of Silence

Brenda lee

False

The Temptations 27 The Four Tops 21

They are all ordained ministers in the church

The Supremes

Pictures: Manfred Mann, The Four Tops, Bob Dylan and Brenda Lee

Answers to Seventies Quiz

Bruce wrote Barry's big hit, I Write The Songs

Elton John & Paul McCartney

True

Just, Show Me The Way to Go in 1977

Hot Love, Get It on, Telegram Sam & Metal Guru

Jimmy Osmond

Perry Como

True, Space Oddity

Never

Never

Answers to Eighties Quiz

The Tourists

Whitney Houston

Queen's Greatest Hits

George Michael & Sheena Easton

The Smiths

Shakin' Stevens

Wham!

Naomi Campbell

Frankie Goes to Hollywood

Cliff Richard

Pictures: The Tourists, Culture Club, Cliff and a FGTH t-shirt

Stars and Their Homes

1. Madonna

2. Elton John

2. Brian May

4. George Harrison

5. Keith Richards

6. Tom Jones

7. Mick Jagger

Answers to Nineties Quiz

Everything But The Girl

Everything I Do I Do It For You (Bryan Adams) & Love is All Around (Wet, Wet, Wet)

Cliff Richard

Geri Halliwell with 4

Shirley Bassey

Steps with 7

Janet Jackson

Take That

Gary Barlow with 9, Jagger & Jackson have 7 each

Westlife

Yet more Stars and Their Homes

1. Eric Clapton

2. Ringo Starr

2. John Entwhistle

4. Rod Stewart

5. George Harrison

6. Robin Gibb

7. Elvis